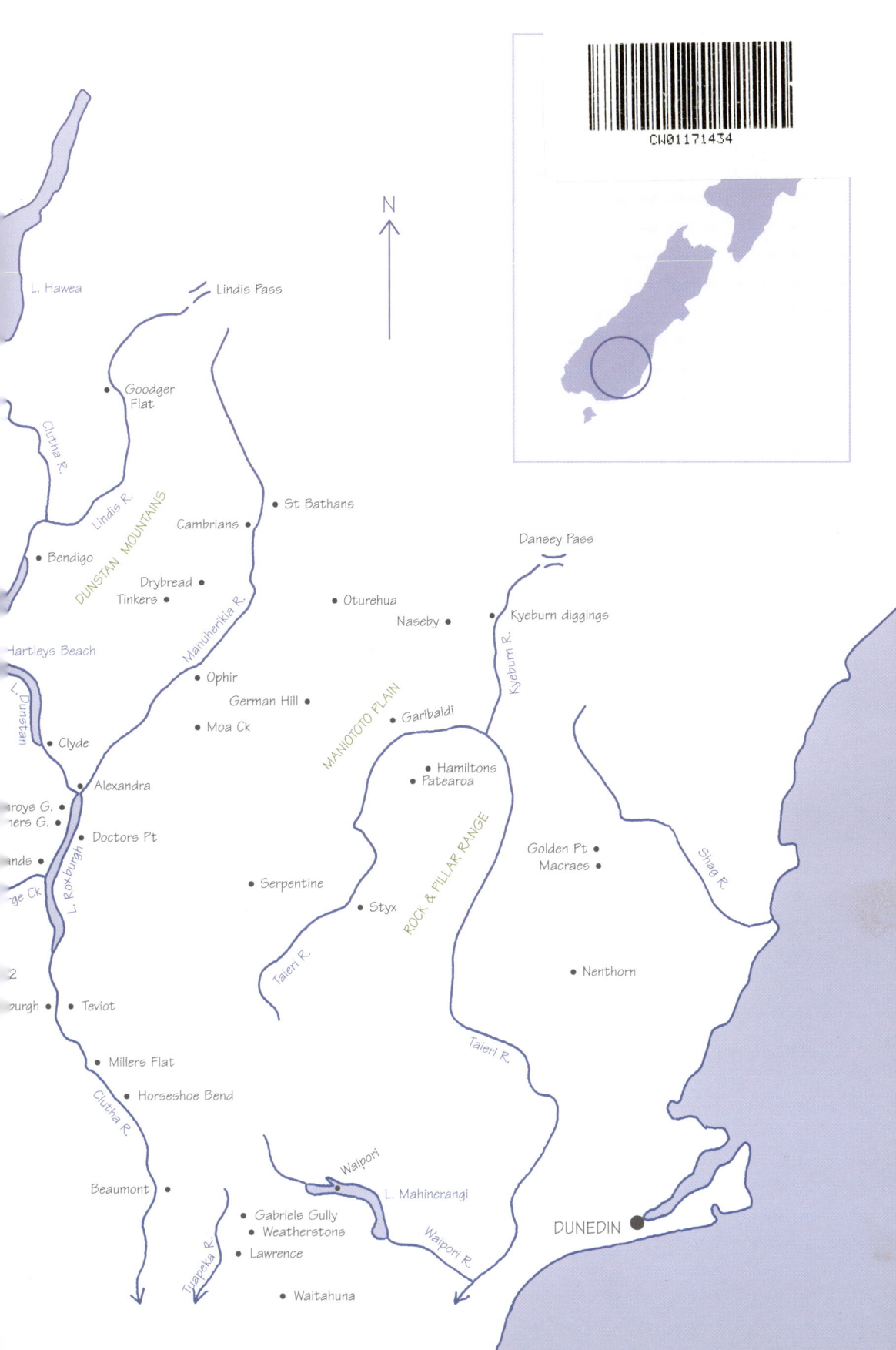

Goldfields of Otago

The tiny town of Dunedin prior to the gold rush to Otago. Painting by J. T. Thomson in 1856. *Hall-Jones family*

Goldfields of Otago
an illustrated history

John Hall-Jones

Also by John Hall-Jones

Early Fiordland, 1968
Mr Surveyor Thomson, 1971
The Invercargill Rotary Club, 1974
Bluff Harbour, 1976
Fiordland Explored, 1976
The Invercargill Club, 1979
Fiordland Place Names, 1979
The South Explored, 1979
An Early Surveyor in Singapore, 1980
New Zealand's Majestic Wilderness, 1981
Goldfields of the South, 1982
Pioneers of Te Anau, 1983
The Thomson Paintings of the Straits Settlements, 1983
Glimpses into Life in Malayan Lands, 1984
Doubtfull Harbour, 1984
The Catlins Guidebook, 1985
Jonathan White's New Zealand, 1986
Martins Bay, 1987
Supplement to Doubtfull Harbour, 1988
Footsteps in the Wilderness, 1989
Discover the South, 1991
John Turnbull Thomson: First Surveyor-General, 1992
Stewart Island Explored, 1994
The Horsburgh Lighthouse, 1995
Discover Fiordland, 1997
Milford Sound, 2000
The Fjords of Fiordland, 2002
Fiordland Place Names, (Revised Edition) 2003

Published by Craig Printing Co. Ltd, P.O. Box 99, Invercargill, New Zealand.

© John Hall-Jones

This book is copyright. Except for the purposes of fair reviewing no part of this publication, including photographs, maps and drawings may be reproduced or transmitted in any form or by any means, electronic or mechanical, including photocopying, recording or by any information storage and retrieval system, without permission in writing from the publisher.

ISBN 0-908629-61-3

Printed and distributed by Craig Printing Co. Ltd,
122 Yarrow Street, P.O. Box 99, Invercargill, New Zealand.
Email: sales@craigprint.co.nz Website: www.craigprint.co.nz

Contents

Introduction & Acknowledgements   7

Chapter		*Page*
1	The Earliest Reports of Gold	9
2	Gabriels Gully	16
3	The Dunstan Rush	34
4	All Roads lead to Dunstan	57
5	Through the Dunstan Gorge	68
6	Bannockburn and the Nevis	74
7	The Rich Reefs of Bendigo	86
8	The Dry Cardrona	94
9	The Golden Arrow	101
10	The Richest River in the World	115
11	The Kawarau Dam	134
12	The Maniototo Goldfields	143
13	The New Zealand Dredge	168

Index   179

Dedication

To the old-timers of yesteryear

Introduction & Acknowledgements

A visitor to Otago in 1860 would have seen Dunedin as a straggling little village of a mere 2,000 people, where in wet weather the streets became a muddy quagmire to pedestrians, horses and bullocks, so much so that the town became known as Mudedin. Within a year the discovery of gold in inland Otago totally transformed Dunedin and the province.

There had been reports of gold in the interior of the province by Maori, explorers and even the provincial surveyors, but these were suppressed by the conservative Superintendent of Otago, Captain William Cargill, who feared that a major gold rush would lead to "mischievous results". He had heard stories from California and Victoria of turbulent mining camps full of harlots, swindlers, gamblers, sly-grog sellers and even murderers. But prodded by a petition from the public, who were concerned about the loss of the labouring population of Otago to other goldfields in New Zealand, the Otago Provincial Council reluctantly agreed to offer a reward of 500 pounds to the discoverer of a remunerative goldfield in Otago.

On 24 May 1861 Gabriel Read, an experienced Tasmanian prospector, followed up a small branch of the Tuapeka River near the future town of Lawrence, where he shovelled away the gravel to see the gold "shining like the stars of Orion on a dark frosty night". It was a memorable day in the history of Otago. From the poorest province in the young colony it was to become the richest. Read was granted the reward of 500 pounds and word quickly spread in and beyond New Zealand of his fabulous find in Gabriels Gully.

The gold rush to Otago had started. "The provincial council was sitting at the time of Read's report", writes Chief Surveyor J. T. Thomson "but it dissolved and a regular 'stampede' took place from all quarters including the councillors. Only women and children were left in the towns and villages." Labourers, tradesmen, professionals, everyone joined in the mass exodus from Dunedin. An endless line of diggers heading for Gabriels Gully, some pushing hand barrows, others laden with swags, shovels and pans. As the news spread prospectors poured in from Australia, California and Europe. The population of Otago rocketed.

On 15 August 1862 two Californian prospectors, Hartley and Reilly, dumped a bag of gold weighing 87 pounds on the counter of the gold receiver in Dunedin. They had an amazing story to tell. Working away with only a tin dish and shovel at the edge of the Clutha River during the winter, when the river was unusually low, they had quietly accumulated their fabulous bag of gold. After being promised a reward of 2,000 pounds, they revealed the location of their discovery as in the Dunstan Gorge, just below the confluence of the Clutha and Kawarau Rivers, soon to become the site of Cromwell.

"87 POUNDS WEIGHT of GOLD"! So ran the headlines, large and bold, in the newspaper next day. Another mass exodus from Dunedin followed, with everyone downing tools, closing shops and setting off inland to reap the golden harvest. The new Dunstan goldfield was declared and almost immediately the banks of the Clutha River were dotted with miners' tents.

With the thawing of snow in the spring of

1862 came the great flood, driving the miners away from the river beaches up into the surrounding hills, where new goldfields were discovered in Conroys Gully, Campbells Creek, Potters, Bannockburn and the Nevis Valley.

As prospectors pushed their way further up the Clutha River and its Kawarau branch, more new goldfields were discovered at Bendigo and Cardrona. Near the head of the Kawarau River, fabulously rich strikes were made in the two main tributaries, the Shotover and the Arrow Rivers.

Instant towns sprang up at Clyde, Alexandra and Cromwell. Queenstown sprouted beside Rees' station at Queenstown Bay on Lake Wakatipu and Arrowtown erupted where the Arrow River spills out of the Arrow Gorge.

Until the autumn of 1863, all the discoveries of gold were in the catchment of the Clutha River. Then in March 1863 gold was discovered in Moa Creek, near Poolburn, by miners streaming over the newly formed Dunstan Road on their way to the Dunstan rush. Two months later gold was found near the future town of Naseby in the Maniototo. Miners rushed into the Manuherikia Valley and the Maniototo Plain, prospecting the mountainous flanks to trigger off a whole series of new discoveries, with the subsequent eruption of a multitude of satellite gold towns. Miners approaching the Maniototo by the Taieri Valley found gold at Hyde, Hamiltons and Serpentine, near the head of the Taieri River.

At the beginning of the Otago gold rush there were only 300 Europeans living in Central Otago. By the end of 1865 the population had soared to 24,000. All nationalities were represented. A party of Cornishmen settled at Moa Creek, Welshmen at Welshmens Gully (Cambrians), the Irish at St Bathans and Italians at Garibaldi. Later Chinese moved in to take over when the Europeans moved out, forming their own Chinese 'camps'.

Fascinated by the story of Otago's gold rush I determined to learn more about its goldfields. I joined the New Zealand Archaeological Association in 1986 at its annual conference in Cromwell, where, under the guidance of archaeologist Neville Ritchie, we visited a number of goldfields in the Upper Clutha Valley. Later he kindly provided me with a full set of his numerous reports on the subject. My wife, Pamela, and I joined the Otago Goldfields Heritage Trust, which, thanks to its indefatigable organiser, Roberta Laraman, run occasional weekend trips to the various goldfields, with John Douglas as guide. Pamela also rode and trekked on ten of the Trusts's cavalcades, passing through many of the more remote goldfields.

During the 1980s, I tramped into most of the goldfields with my old tramping mate Bruce Miles, photographing the old gold batteries, gold workings and miners huts. I was glad I did so, as on revisiting them recently we found that some of the batteries had since collapsed or rotted away. Fortuitously I now had a record of what they used to look like. I also took along Chief Surveyor J. T. Thomson's early paintings of the goldfields in the 1860s, lining them up with the present-day scene. I then extended my search for early pictures of the goldfields to the local museums at Arrowtown, Alexandra, Lawrence and Naseby, the collections at the Hocken Library, Otago Settlers Museum and the Alexander Turnbull Library, to all I am deeply indebted.

By now I had accumulated a very large collection of photographs and paintings of the Otago goldfields, many of which have never been published before. I felt suitably armed to proceed with an overall illustrated history of the Otago goldfields along similar lines to my earlier illustrated history of the goldfields of Southland, *Goldfields of the South*. In doing so I am indebted to a number of people who have helped me with my research, including the above already mentioned. In particular I wish to thank the late Peter Chandler who generously shared his meticulously researched knowledge of the goldfields with me. I will never forget his field day with my wife and I to the old diggings at Potters No. 2 and Campbells Creek on the Old Man Range. Ron Murray, the authority on the Cromwell, Bannockburn and Nevis Valley areas, who generously provided me with a number of important photographs. A number of authors of specific books and reports on the goldfields, whose names are acknowledged in the relevant parts of the text and the reference sections at the end of each chapter. My wife, who accompanied me through the Nevis Valley twice, she riding her horse, Suellen, I walking, and who later meticulously checked through the text of the manuscript.

Finally I wish to thank my publishers, Craig Printing Company Limited, for all their care and attention in producing such a handsome, well-printed book.

CHAPTER 1
The Earliest Reports of Gold

*Gold was found in the Clutha River above the junction of the Manuherikia
and in the Tuapeka Stream in sufficient quantities
to make it probable that it would pay to work.*
Alexander Garvie, 1858

The Maori were aware of the occurrence of gold in the great Matau (Clutha) River, but unlike the European they were not plagued with money matters, nor could they see any practical use for such a soft metal.

The great southern chief, Tuhawaiki, told the whaler, William Palmer, that "plenty of 'whereo' [yellow] stone, such as that of the watch-seals of white men were made, was to be found on the river beaches inland, and that the Matau River was the place where it principally occurred".[1]

Other Maori volunteered similar statements, when they observed the value that the newcomers seemed to place upon their golden coins and ornaments. One Maori, Rakiraki, who had lived at Wanaka, told Thomas Archibald of how he had "once picked up a piece of gold about the size of a small potato on the bank of the Molyneux [Captain Cook's name for the Clutha], but did not know its [monetary] value and threw it into the river. They had seen the gold on the sides of the river, where their canoes had been lying."[1]

In the hope of discovering an El Dorado, Thomas Archibald set off up the Clutha in a whaleboat with a party of five in March 1852. "We prospected the bars and banks of the river as far as a creek now named the Beaumont"[1], he reported later to Vincent Pyke, by then Secretary of the Otago Goldfields. "As none of us [except a Californian miner] knew anything about gold-seeking and getting nothing more than colour, we returned [downriver] after nearly three weeks. If our Californian miner had been the practical hand he represented himself to be, I have no doubt we would have been successful in getting a good prospect."

Gold was spotted by the early settlers in many parts of the province, but the reports were suppressed as they were considered as being likely to lead to "mischevious results"[1]. In October 1851 the two explorers, Pharazyn and Charles Nairn, sent some specimens of quartz gold to Dunedin, that they had picked up from Charles Suisted's property at Goodwood, North Otago. "We send the specimens", writes Nairn,[1] "under the impression that the prompt communication of the discovery will be of importance to the Otago settlement."

But the conservative Superintendent of Otago, Captain William Cargill, was not desirous that his little community should be diverted from the even

Rakiraki of Wanaka who told the early Europeans of the gold he had seen in the Clutha River. A. Anderson

The explorer Charles Nairn who found gold at Goodwood, north of Dunedin in 1851. *C. Nairn*

Captain William Cargill, the conservative Superintendent of Otago. Painting by J. T. Thomson. *Hall-Jones family*

tenure of its way. Likewise, the editor of the newspaper sagely cautioned the people against leaving their ordinary occupations, concluding a leader on the subject with a few extra words of wisdom, "Flour is more necessary than gold, and may be more profitable."!

In 1856 Surveyor-General Charles Ligar reported gold in the gravel and sand of the Mataura River. "If Charles Ligar had thrown dynamite in its most diabolical form into Superintendent Cargill's office, it is questionable whether he would have caused greater consternation," comments Vincent Pyke.[1] "Captain Cargill appears to have had a very lively, and perhaps altogether unnatural dislike to goldfields, 'diggers' and everything connected therewith."

When Ligar's letter was presented to the provincial council the determined Cargill countered that gold had been found for years in the Auckland and Nelson provinces, "but had been quite unremunerative". But the evidence was to the contrary. Nelson had done well from its gold rush. After pondering over the subject the public of Otago presented a petition to the council on 4 November 1857 pointing out that "many of the labouring population [of Otago] had already left the province for the Nelson Goldfields" and many more men were preparing to do so, to the serious loss of the province. "The existence of gold in the province is a well-ascertained fact", the petitioners argued, and the council should take immediate steps "towards providing whether gold exists in payable quantities or not. A handsome reward [should be offered] for proof of the existence of a remunerative goldfield within this Province." The petitioners won the day and in a far-reaching decision the council voted that a bonus of 500 pounds would be paid to the discoverer of the remunerative goldfield within the province of Otago.

The surveyors report gold

During his survey of the Clutha River Valley in late 1857 and early 1858 Alexander Garvie found traces of gold in the gravel of several of the streams and rivers:

> "The trials were all made on the very surface, at such odd times as would not interrupt the proper work of the survey, by one of the party, [the botanist artist John Buchanan] who happened to have previously visited the Australian goldfields. The gold found was in every case small and scaly, varying from the smallest specks to about the roughness of bran. It was found *in the Clutha River above the junction of the Manuherikia, and in the Tuapeka stream*, in sufficient quantities to make it probable that it would pay to work if set about in a proper manner, with some wholesale system of washing, such as sluicing. Specks were also found in the *Manuherikia* and *Waitahuna*."

In republishing Garvie's report later, Vincent Pyke added the italics (as above) to emphasise the fact that Garvie had indicated exactly the sites where some of the most famous and profitable of the gold workings were afterwards 'discovered'. In his first official report as Secretary of the Goldfields in 1862 Vincent Pyke wrote:[1]

> "I cannot but regard this as *the first practical demonstration* of the mineral wealth of Otago. Earlier explorers had merely ascertained its existence, yet here was sufficient evidence to have satisfied the most incredulous. The announcement was, however, unheeded at the time, and it was reserved for Mr Gabriel Read and Messrs Hartley and Reilly to develop the hidden treasures of which Mr Garvie undoubtedly intimated the presence, although he was probably unaware of the importance of his discovery."[1]

Writing 24 years later Pyke comments, "I am still at a loss to understand how it was that no effort was made at the time to test the accuracy and value of these early discoveries. Garvie's report [dated 15 July 1858] was published in the *Otago Provincial Gazette* at the end of September. Buried in that respectable periodical it fell dead on the public ear, probably was never seen beyond official circles and no action whatever followed. Yet all the time there was a bonus of 500 pounds proffered for the discovery of a remunerative goldfield!"

In a footnote appended to Garvie's report the Chief Surveyor, J. T. Thomson, added:[3] "the best sample of gold yet brought into town was in the Tokomairiro River (south branch). This sample indicates a workable field. It was shown to me in 1858 by a native of Bombay, Edward Peters [known as Black Peter, because of his colour]." As Peters explained to Thomson in Hindustani (which Thomson could speak), "he was in the habit of washing small quantities of gold from the sands of the river and he gave me an account of his daily earnings and the sites of his discovery."

Peters had found the gold at Glenore, a few kilometres west of Milton, on the current highway to Queenstown. As we shall see later, Peters also found gold in the Tuapeka Stream, before Gabriel Read made his famous 'discovery' in 1861.

Tokomairiro River and Glenore (Woolshed) Valley, where Edward Peters discovered gold in 1858.

A lone rider on the road to Lindis Pass from the Canterbury side. Painting by Nicholas Chevalier in 1866. *National Gallery*

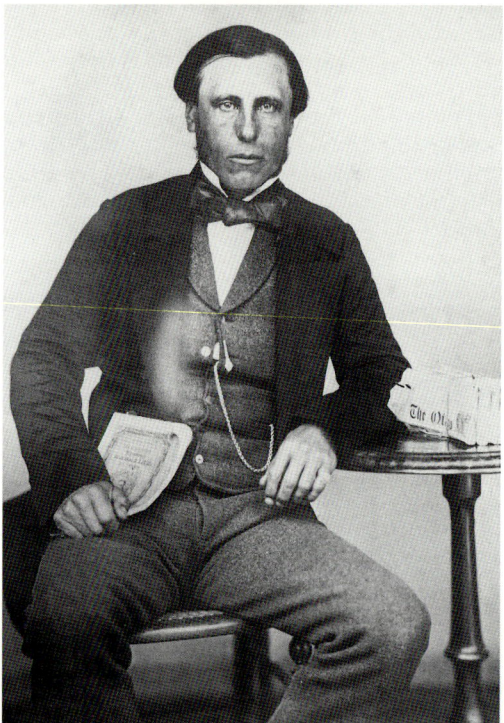

Chief Surveyor J. T. Thomson who discovered gold in the Lindis River, four years before the Lindis rush. *Hall-Jones family*

In December 1857 Thomson made his own discovery of gold during his exploration and survey of Otago. After crossing the Lindis Pass (which he named after Lindisfarne Island)[4] he descended the Lindis Valley, where he discovered gold in the Lindis River.

Thomson reported his discovery of gold in the Lindis River in 1858 (the same year as Garvie's report), but as with Garvie's discovery nothing happened. Maybe if Thomson had applied for the reward of 500 pounds it would have aroused more public interest and someone would have at least gone to check on it. But as Thomson commented later,[3] "even if the ground had proved permanently payable, I, according to goldfield rules [Thomson being an official] would not have got the reward."

It was a whole four years later in 1861, when a road was being constructed across the Lindis Pass for the benefit of the local runholders, that the roadworkers 'rediscovered' the gold in the Lindis River, triggering off the first gold rush in Otago.

The Lindis Rush

It seems strange that it was by accident and not design that Thomson's gold in the Lindis River was 'rediscovered' by a party of roadworkers in March 1861. It also seems a little odd that Otago's first workable goldfield should be reported by the *Lyttelton Times*[5] of Canterbury and not an Otago newspaper:

> "A party of men, employed in road-making by the Otago Government, picked up some nuggets in the River Lindis, a tributary of the Molyneux [Clutha], where they were engaged making cuttings for the main road to cross. Mr McLean ['Big' John McLean of Morven Hills run] on whose run the gold was found, saw some gold in possession of one of the men. It weighed about 4oz, and consisted of some waterworn nuggets from the size of a grain of wheat to that of a bean, and apparently of a very fine quality . . . As the stream where the gold was found is small, and close to the hills, it offers no prospect for a large field sufficient to induce diggers to proceed there from any distance at this time of the year."

When the *Otago Witness* eventually caught up with the big news it described the goldfield

Washing for gold in a sluice box (Long Tom). The heavy gold is trapped by riffle bars and matting.
Alexander Turnbull Library.

Left: Washing for gold with a cradle. A two-handed job, pouring water on paydirt with one hand, while rocking the cradle with the other to sieve the gold.
Alexander Turnbull Library

as being "70-90 miles from Dunedin, the precise locality is quite a mystery".[1] Actually the location was in the Lindis Valley at Goodger Flat.

Amongst the roadworkers were some men who had prospected on the Australian goldfields and "it was in the prosecution of their labours [in the Lindis Valley] that they found gold scattered through the soil and subsequently discovered it in the sands of the streams".[1]

In spite of the onset of an early winter with snow conditions, there "was a rush of 300 prospectors to the 'diggings' which reached a maximum population of 400".[1] Describing the field in April 1861 Robert Booth (with his companion Legge) wrote:[6]

> "The banks of the river were crowded with men at work; some in the water, some out; others pitching tents or tending horses; some slapping together rough tables or cradles and Long Toms for washing gold. Scores of horses were tethered among the tents and in the open. Above all was the constant buzz of many men about their business. By 17 April three hundred men could be found already on the diggings, many of whom came from Canterbury. At one stage there were said to have been five hundred men on the field."

Booth and Legge's dwelling measured "10 by 12 feet with sod walls". Their greatest discomfort was caused by rats, which

The Lindis Hotel in 1902. Note hitching posts in front. *G. Duff*

The substantial ruins of the Lindis Hotel today. Note massive chimneys.

descended at night like myriads of "Assyrians". Sometimes they worked all day for "five shillings worth of gold".

Letters[1] began to appear in the press nominating various miners for the "bonus" offered for the discovery of a "remunerative field". One nomination undersigned by 40 diggers in Lindis Valley, certified that "Samuel McIntyre was the first discoverer of this goldfield and that he was entitled to the reward". Interestingly two of the signatories, William Docherty (later the famous prospector in Dusky Sound) and John Falconer, were also nominated for the reward. In a supporting letter Edward McGlashan wrote: "Two men, Docherty and Falconer, who have been working here for several weeks, assure me that they have averaged over an ounce a day each." Others testified to the value of the field including one provincial councillor who wrote enthusiastically: "The country in every direction is literally teaming with gold." Even the new Superintendent of Otago "thought it likely some thousands would be attracted to the Lindis Pass diggings after the winter".

In spite of these wild claims the earlier forecast of the *Lyttelton Times* proved to be correct. The field was an exceedingly limited one and by July it had been virtually worked out. When the Danish prospector George Hassing visited the field in the summer of 1861, he found "only a few isolated parties ground-sluicing in the riverbed. The store kept by Mr Hassall has closed down. The diggers have cleared out for the new field at Gabriels Gully", Hassing records.[7]

Fortuitously the council had postponed the decision of paying a bonus to the 'discoverers' of the Lindis field. By July their claims were totally eclipsed and overshadowed by the discovery in Gabriels Gully.

Nevertheless, for many years after the abortive rush of 1861 small parties of miners laboured on at Goodger Flat with modest returns.[8] Some sluicing was done on the terraces on the right bank of the river and during the 1890s Chinese miners thoroughly did over the whole riverbed of the flat by wing-damming. In 1901 a dredge worked the flat about a kilometre down from the Lindis Hotel. During the depression years of the 1930s there was a renewal of mining activity in the Camp Creek area near the hotel.

The hotel had its genesis as a slygrog shop at the height of the Lindis rush. Then in 1873 a permanent hotel with a licence was built on the site to cope with the growing tourist traffic over the pass. In 1911 several bedrooms and a new dining room were added. Later the Cormick family ran the hotel for 21 years for buses and travellers over the pass. There was also a post office and store attached for the convenience of the local miners. After the highway switched to the opposite side of the river the hotel was abandoned. Today the substantial ruins of the Lindis Hotel can be found at the head of Old Faithful Road (the old Lindis Pass Road) at Goodger Flat.

REFERENCES
1. Pyke, Vincent, *Early Gold Discoveries in Otago*, 1887
2. Garvie, A., *Report on the Reconnaissance survey of SE Otago, Otago Prov. Gaz.*, 1858, Vol 3, p279.
3. Thomson, J. T., *Original Exploration in Otago*, 1878.
4. Hall-Jones, John, *John Turnbull Thomson*, 1992
5. *Lyttelton Times*, April 1861.
6. Roxburgh, Irvine, *Wanaka Story*, 1977
7. Hassing, George, *The Memory Log of G. M. Hassing*, 1929
8. Duff, Geoffrey, *Sheep may safely graze*, 1978.

Miners' camp near Camp Creek, 1934. Lindis River behind. *G. Duff*

CHAPTER 2
Gabriels Gully

*I saw the gold shining like the stars in Orion
on a dark frosty night.*
Gabriel Read, 1861

Not enough credit has been given to Edward Peters, whose pioneer prospecting led to the opening of the Gabriels Gully goldfield, a fabulously rich field which was to completely change the whole future of Otago.

After showing his samples from the Tokomairiro River to Chief Surveyor J. T. Thomson in 1858, "the best sample yet brought into town", Peters moved inland to Evans Flat where he took on a labouring job on Edmund Bowler's Tuapeka run. In his spare time Peters continued his "habit" of panning for gold along the banks of the Tuapeka River, which ran through Evans Flat. He did so well that his success became quite widely known. An honest soul, he thought nothing of keeping his secret to himself. On a visit to Balclutha he told the Clutha River ferryman, John Thomson,[1] of his success. Thomson was so impressed that he walked back with Peters to Evans Flat, where he saw that the story was true.

John Thomson teamed up with Peters and soon they were joined by an American Negro. The trio prospected in and around Evans Flat for six months or so, finding "the colour" everywhere they went. But they lacked experience and were unsuccessful in keeping their diggings free of water or saving the gold sufficiently well in their cradle. As John Thomson recalled later, "I believe we lost more than we gained".[1]

The source of the gold which Peters discovered at Evans Flat was the fabulously rich Blue Spur, between the heads of Munros and Gabriels Streams. If only Peters had been an experienced prospector he would have followed up either of these branches of the Tuapeka River and struck the rich mother lode. But this was to be left to the competent Gabriel Read.

Following Read's discovery of the gold in Gabriels Gully, John Thomson took up a good claim in the gully, but Peters apparently forsook the field. He was nominated for the bonus at least twice.[1] One letter, dated 8 July 1861, has a laconic note attached to it: "Received 12 July 1861. Disposed of."

Many years later, in 1885, some tardy measure of justice was accorded to Peters when a conscience-smitten government offered him a grant of 50 pounds, on the condition that the public subscribed the same amount. A sympathetic public matched the grant and by "judicious investment" a cottage was obtained for him at Port Molyneux, where he lived until his health failed. He

Edward Peters, the Hindu labourer who discovered gold in the Tokomairiro River in 1858 and afterwards in the Tuapeka River.
Hocken Library

Gabriels Gully 17

George Munro outside his shepherd's hut in Munros Gully. *Gabriels Gully Jubilee booklet*

Right: Gabriel Read who, in 1861, discovered the rich gold in Gabriels Gully that triggered off the gold rush to Otago. *Otago Settlers Museum*

was moved to the Benevolent Institution in Dunedin where he died in June 1893. So ended the life of Edward Peters, the luckless pioneer of the first great gold rush in New Zealand.

Gabriel Read

The contrast between Edward Peters and Gabriel Read could not have been greater. The former was an uneducated Hindu labourer, the latter was the well-educated son of a prosperous landowner in Tasmania. Most importantly, Read had taken part in both the California and Victoria gold rushes and by the time he came to New Zealand he was a thoroughly competent prospector.

Gabriel Read was attracted to Otago by Charles Ligar's report of gold in the Mataura River, but by the time Read landed in Dunedin in early 1861 the report had proved to be a 'fizzer'. Nevertheless he continued to Tokomairiro (Milton) where he fell in with John Hardy, a provincial councillor, on whose farm he worked for a couple of months. Hardy was a born optimist who never wavered in his belief that payable gold would be found 'somewhere about here' and that it would lift Otago out of the doldrums.[1] At a political meeting in Tokomairiro, Read met another man of influence, John L. Gillies, who strongly urged him to prospect the Tuapeka country where "Black Peter" had only been "hen-scratching". With further encouragement from the optimistic Hardy, Read set forth for the Tuapeka country about 23 May 1861.[1] Initially he spent four hours prospecting in the Waitahuna River with "satisfactory results". Then he made for Evans Flat where he found alluvial gold "widely distributed". Later that day he moved up Munros Stream to the head of Munros Gully, where he met a shepherd, George Munro, who told him all about "Black Peter's" workings and insisted on Read staying the night in his shepherd's hut. The events of the following day were so important for

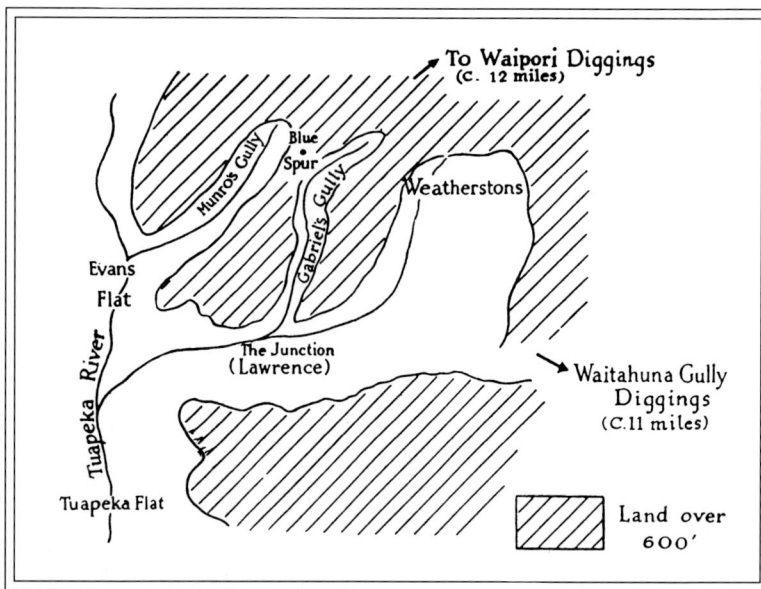

Sketch map of the Gabriels Gully area. *W. R. Mayhew*

the future of Tuapeka and Otago that they are best told in his own words:[1]

"We were up betimes in the morning, breakfast dispatched, we followed the ridge and struck on the Gabriel's branch at the top of the hill where the beech forest was thick, the stream rocky and insignificant, and banks lined with the gnarled roots of the forest, and here I thanked him for his hospitality and parted . . . I followed the creek down till I got on the flat, and saw no favourable opportunity of trying a prospect for some time. The drift was deep and cumbered with boulders and little or no loose gold lower down. Getting opposite the Blue Spur, the prospects began to brighten, just when I had deemed it meet to make a flit for my tent, as darkness was fast coming on the scene. At a place where a kind of road crossed on a shallow bar, I shovelled away about 2½ feet of gravel, arrived at a beautiful soft slate and saw the gold shining like the stars in Orion on a dark frosty night."

The following day Read prospected all the way down the gully, then over a low ridge to the east to the future Weatherstons. After this thorough search he concluded that "these hills must be more or less auriferous".

The excitement he created back at John Hardy's farm can well be imagined. On 4 June Read wrote an historic letter to the then Superintendent of Otago, Major John Richardson:[3]

Tokomairiro, 4th June, 1861
To Major Richardson, &c.,

Sir, – I take the liberty of troubling you with a short report on the result of a gold prospecting tour which I commenced about a fortnight since, and which occupied me about ten days. During that period I travelled inland about thirty-five miles, and examined the ravines and tributaries of the Waitahuna and Tuapeka Rivers.

My equipment consisted of a tent, blankets, spade, tin dish, butcher's knife, and about a week's provisions. I examined a large area of country and washed pans of earth in different localities. I found at many places prospects which would hold out a certainty that men with the proper tools would be munificently remunerated – and in one place, for ten hours' work with pan and butcher's knife, I was enabled to collect about seven ounces of gold.

I have now had constructed proper machinery and tools, and will be able in the course of a few days to report with more certainty. Mr. John Hardy, the Member for this district, will accompany me, and on his return, communicate personally with Your Honour. His earnestness in favour of a goldfields discovery has so pleased me that I have been induced to make him my confidant, and he has kindly placed his time at my disposal.

Had I made anything like an exhibition of my gold, the plain would have been deserted by all the adult inhabitants the next day, and the farmers would have suffered seriously from a neglect of agricultural operations at this season of the year.

Although the being able to work secretly for a time would greatly benefit me, I feel it my duty to impart these facts. To know that the stream of population must set through Waihola rather than Oamaru, I consider it important for you to know. These communications are made in confidence that my secret is safe with Major Richardson, but if a disclosure is of any benefit to the public interest, you are at liberty to treat this as a public communication to the Superintendent. Mr Hardy will be in town in the course of a week, and I think you might perhaps do well to await his return, when he will impart the result of his trip. At all events, I leave myself as a client under Your Honour's patronage, convinced that by so doing I take the most certain course to ensure the benefit to which I may some day be considered entitled for this important discovery.

I have the honour to be,
Your obedient servant,
Thos. Gabriel Read

Read's letter was at first received with incredulity.[3] The news seemed too good to be true. Prospectors had been seeking gold for the past ten years, with many reported discoveries, but only the Lindis field had been substantiated and this was now running out. More evidence was needed.

Meantime, Read had returned to his gully with John Hardy's son, Edwin, and a Yorkshire lad, Brooks, who was employed on the farm. Within a week the trio had won five pounds of gold. John Hardy joined them and on 28 June he addressed an eager council on the results of his investigations. With Gabriel Read he had prospected country "about 31 miles long by 5 broad and in every hole they sank they found the precious metal."[3] This certainly activated the council and Chief Surveyor J. T. Thomson was sent to report on the field. Thomson visited the gully on 1 July:[4]

> "I came up to the place, where about 150 men had already collected. On visiting Read's tents, and telling him my errand, he at once proffered me every explanation, and drawing from beneath his blankets a bag of native gold, he weighed it in my presence, amounting to 9 lbs. 4 oz., the result of fourteen days' work, the party consisting of three. Other miners were equally complacent."

Thomson recorded the returns of both Gabriel's party and the "other miners" in his notebook, dated 1 July 1861, and later copied these onto the back of his painting of Gabriels Gully.[4]

> Gabriel Read (the discoverer, 3 of a party) got 9 pounds 4 ounces in 14 days.
> John Jenkins (5 of a party) got 49 ounces in 4 days.
> John Cargill 5 (3 of a party) got 20 ounces in 4 days.
> James Martin (3 of a party) got half an ounce in 4 hours.
> C & J Lammond (2 of a party) got 2 ounces in 1 day.
> John Cargill (on my going back to him) got 10 ounces in that morning.
> Copied from my notebook of 1 July 1861, J. T. Thomson.

The next morning he added the returns of two more parties before riding back to Dunedin:

> Peter Lindsay's party (3 men), 3 ounces in 3½ days.
> Burnside and J. L. Gillies, 8 ounces in six days.

The remainder of the "150 men" on the field were still in the process of "settling in" and were not yet "seriously at work".

Thomson's,[1] findings were certainly impressive. He presented them to the council on 3 July and the latter released them to the press. The public reaction was electric. Even the normally sober *Otago Witness* exploded in an editorial, "Gold, gold, gold is the universal subject of conversation."

"The council was sitting at the time", writes Thomson,[4] "but it dissolved and a regular 'stampede' took place from all quarters, including the councillors[!] Only women and children were left in the towns and villages. On the first gold escort bringing home 5,056 ounces, the excitement became intense, spreading to Victoria and other parts of Australia [and later California and Europe]."

Labourers, tradesmen, professionals, everyone joined the mass exodus from Dunedin heading out to the Taieri plain, across the Taieri River, over the Maungatua Hill and the bleak Lammerlaw Hills to the diggings.

> "An endless procession of heavy-booted, mud-stained, thirsty wayfarers, tramp, tramp past Peter Robertson's house [head shepherd on the Tuapeka run], tin cans banging, pannikins clattering, waggons and drays lumbering along. There were strange contraptions of wood and rope, termed hand barrows, piled high with swags and tin dishes; wide straggling rows of men of all nations and languages, each man 'humping his bluey' or shouting strange oaths . . . Others toiled on laden with bags of flour, blankets, shovels, spades . . . Tents sprang up as if by magic; wood and calico accommodation houses; stables and huts . . ."[6]

In September 1861 J. T. Thomson returned to Gabriels Gully and painted a view looking towards the head of the gully, the Blue Spur Ridge on the left, the Lammerlaws in the background and the valley leading off to Weatherstons on the right. The formal-looking tent, with flagstaff alongside, is the 'government building', a tent which served both the warden (Major Croker) and as a 'courthouse', when required. Down in the gully are the huts and tents of the miners at work. On the skyline of the Blue Spur Ridge is the nucleus of the definitive town of Blue

J. T. Thomson's painting of Gabriels Gully in September 1861, the earliest known painting of the gold rush. View looking towards the head of the gully, with Blue Spur ridge on the left and the warden's tent in the foreground. *Hall-Jones family*

Photograph in the 1860s looking back down the gully towards the original town of Lawrence at the entrance. Blue Spur Road on right. *E. M. Lovell-Smith*

J. T. Thomson's painting in 1861 of the "endless line" of diggers descending off the Lammerlaw Hills towards the tents and smoke in Gabriels Gully. Weatherstons Gully to the left, Munros Gully to the right. *Hall-Jones family*

Spur. The painting is complementary to an early photograph looking back down the gully towards the original town of Lawrence, which is forming at the entrance to the gully. The road in the foreground is the original Blue Spur Road.

One of the most vivid descriptions of the settlement at Gabriels Gully in 1861 comes from the pen of an English miner, C. L. Money:

> "Here were canvas and galvanised iron stores, public houses, restaurants, shanties of all descriptions and with every conceivable name, scattered around in all directions; while advertisements of nigger minstrels, gold buyers' prices and placards, were flaunting everywhere." His first night there he slept on a slab bench in a stable, "a couple of blankets and a corner of a bench being considered a lucky claim." Opposite this stable was a "calico store some seven or eight feet high, and about ten or twelve in area; a few planks from old brandy and gin cases, nailed on saplings driven into the ground, formed the counter, on which were heaped the principal ingredients of a digger's domestic requirements – viz. sides of bacon, a tub or so of butter, one or two dry cheeses, sardines, lobsters, salmon, and other potted fishes and meats, bread, tobacco, clay pipes, and piled-up boxes of Litchford's Vesta matches. The whole of this extensive warehouse was about as large as a reasonably sized dog-kennel, and had an apartment behind, separated from the front shop by an almost transparent piece of calico. [This was the gambling den], with six men seated around an old gin case deep in unlimited loo."

J. T. Thomson leaves us a little watercolour sketch of the "endless line" of diggers descending off the Lammerlaws towards Gabriels Gully, the smoke rising from the settlement. Many of these 'hopefuls' were totally ignorant of gold-mining methods. To these inexperienced men Gabriel Read gave generously of his knowledge. At a meeting of miners on 7 July he spoke on how to work the ground properly and also advised them to form a committee to control the field until a warden was appointed. A committee was duly elected, with John L. Gillies as chairman. A deeply religious man, Read donated 50 pounds towards the provision of Sunday services. "I felt I had been His agent and took the course which had led to the present results", he wrote.[3]

On 19 July Read set out with Captain William Baldwin (a runholder, who also had

Goldfields of Otago

a claim at Gabriels Gully) to prospect the Waitahuna Gully, some kilometres away. Although they found gold there on 20 July and there was a rush to this gully, Waitahuna was never the same success as Gabriels Gully.

On 4 November Read was awarded the bonus of 500 pounds for the discovery of a payable field in Otago. In May 1862 he was granted an extra 500 pounds in recognition of the great benefits his discovery had brought to Otago. From the poorest province in the young colony, Otago had become the richest. Read drifted back to Hobart where he died in 1894.

Weatherstons

Two brothers were not doing well at their claim at Gabriels Gully and were running out of tucker. One day in July they set out over the low ridge to the east at the head of the gully, on a pig-hunt. They struck it lucky and shot two pigs in the valley below. Leaving one pig concealed in the tussocks, they carried the other one back to Gabriels Gully, where they sold it for food. Next day the brothers returned to the valley to collect the other pig, taking a pick and shovel with them to do a little prospecting in the stream in the valley. Digging a hole on the river flat, they obtained several ounces of gold.

The movements of the two brothers had not gone unnoticed. Men began to 'shadow'

Miners' monument in Waitahuna Gully, where Gabriel Read and Captain William Baldwin discovered gold on 20 July 1861.

Weatherstons in the mid-1860s. *Hocken library*

Weatherstons Black Horse brewery, 1897. *Hocken Library*

Right: Remains of the brewery, 1979

them. Then "one morning the miners were coming over the spur into the gully like a swarm of bees". The Weatherstons rush was on. For that was the name of the two brothers, David and John Weatherston. The name has been spelt variously on maps and signposts as Wetherston, Weatherstone and even Watherston. But in a definitive letter to the *Otago Daily Times* on 15 March 2005 Barbara Weatherston Stewart points out that the correct spelling of the family name is Weatherston. As such this spelling must now be accepted.

Weatherstons developed rapidly into a real rip-roaring mining town, the largest population (said to be 5,000[8]) on the goldfield at the time. There were "fourteen hotels, dancing saloons, numerous gambling dens, and every kind of moneymaking establishment the inhabitants could think of".[2] Many of the miners were from Victoria, as witnessed by the names of the streets laid out, Collins, Bourke and Elizabeth, all borrowed from Melbourne and of course

Elevators working in the huge sluiced basin at the head of Gabriels Gully, 1900. Jagged remains of the ridge between Gabriels Gully and Munros Gully on the skyline. Ridge leading up to Blue Spur on left. *Hocken Library*

there was a Ballarat Hotel. Beer was first brewed behind the shaving saloon in 1863. By 1866 the Black Horse brewery was producing "prime ale". Due partly to the quality of the Weatherstons Stream and of course the brewer's skill, Black Horse beer became famous from Canterbury to Bluff and continued in production right up till 1923.

During an equivalent period of four weeks in November 1861 Weatherstons was reported as producing more gold than Gabriels Gully. Some of the miners were returning six ounces of gold a week. Then in August 1862, as quickly as it had mushroomed, the town became virtually deserted. The Dunstan rush had started.

The Blue Spur

The rich gold in Gabriels Gully was derived from the blue-grey conglomerate of the spur between Gabriels and Munros Gullies. Flint-hard in consistency, the miners referred to it as blue "cement". Heavily impregnated with gold this "cement" had been laid down millions of years ago.

At first the gold seemed to be there for the taking as the miners washed the "cement" in the gully at the foot of the spur. Then as the alluvial gold ran out they began attacking the Blue Spur itself, using a sequence of techniques.[7]

1. Initially by mining. The first shaft was sunk in 1862 on the crest of the Blue Spur. Other mines were driven, mainly on the Munros

Gully side, to keep clear of the sluicing in Gabriels Gully.

2. By 1862 water races were being constructed (from as far afield as the Waipori River) to bring in water for ground sluicing. But this was not very successful so . . .

3. Blasting powder was introduced to break down the "cement" and this greatly assisted the sluicing operations.

4. In 1874 the first of seven "cement" crushing batteries was erected and by the 1900s almost the entire bottom layer (the good payable strata) had been removed and crushed.

5. During 1879 J. R. Perry introduced the Californian hydraulic elevating technique (the first time it was used in New Zealand) for raising sluiced material under pressure and running it back down over gold-saving tables.

6. In 1888 the giant Consolidated Goldmining Company amalgamated all other companies and reworked the accumulated tailing on the floor of Gabriels Gully, elevating them for the next 25 years.

With all these methods of attack the changes in the Blue Spur were spectacular indeed. A large part of the Spur was removed, leaving a great ampitheatre at the head of the gully. A deep layer of tailings (in some places 45 metres deep) formed a new gully floor, covering all vestiges of the initial gold rush. Today, the Department of Conservation (DOC) has an interesting walkway around this great sluiced basin at the head of Gabriels Gully, with information panels pointing out the relics of the various mining techniques.

During the great depression years of the 1930s, would-be prospectors camped in the gully, seeking gold with pick, shovel, cradle and pan, just as their predecessors did in the 1860s.

The towns

The original 'commercial centre' in Gabriels Gully was at "Gibraltar", about halfway up the gully at the foot of the Blue Spur. A small 'canvas town', it was the 'shopping centre' for the miners, with an array of stores and hotels. Then as the tailings accumulated in the floor of the gully the 'township' shifted up the hillside to form the new town of Blue Spur. In its heyday,[8] Blue Spur had two hotels, two churches, a school and a variety of shops. The original road to Blue Spur, up and along the ridge summit, is still in use today. There was no proper road along the gully floor and all supplies to the miners had to be sledged down the steep hillside from the town. A steep track, known as Jacobs Ladder, also linked Blue Spur with the gully below.

The original town of Lawrence was at the mouth of Gabriels Gully. Situated at the junction of Gabriels and Weatherstons Streams it was known as "The Junction". Then it shifted a little east to become the present town of Lawrence.

About a kilometre west of "The Junction", on the righthand side of the current highway to Queenstown, was the Chinese "camp" as it was called.

Lawrence's Chinatown

Lawrence's Chinatown was founded in 1867[11] after the Lawrence Town Council declared all Chinese residences and shops as 'out of bounds' within the town boundaries. Being on the 'gateway' to the Otago goldfields it was to become the largest Chinatown in Otago, with a population of 123[11] in 1891. Early reports describe it as a "conglomeration of buildings wedged a trifle too closely together". But as Dr James Ng[11] points out, after it was surveyed in 1882 (when 26 sections and streets were laid out) the quality of the buildings improved considerably. Its resident population included important merchants, the best Chinese doctors, various tradesmen

Blue Spur township with Jacobs Ladder leading down to the elevators in the "big hole" at the head of Gabriels Gully. *Hocken Library*

McKenzie's old store and post office on the Blue Spur Road today.

and shopkeepers. The premises included several big stores, two joss houses, an immigration barracks for newcomers, the Chinese Empire Hotel, boarding houses, eating places, opium and gambling dens and residences. This mix of places was the most extensive of all Chinese towns in New Zealand.

The early "camp" was described by a newspaper reporter in 1869:

"Its sheets of corrugated galvanised iron and flitches of weather-boarding are essentially that of a diggings township in its early stage of existence. A closer inspection, however, brings out the foreign element in its broadest aspect. The hieroglyphical tracings on the signboards, the outlandish gibberish spoken, the hook-nosed shoes and broad-brimmed hats all making the visitor feel as if he is a stranger in [his own] land.

"There are one or two general stores with stocks as large as any [European counterpart]. The principal days for transacting business are Saturdays and Sundays when John Chinaman comes into the 'camp' to stock up for the ensuing week. At the conclusion of his purchases the storekeeper 'shouts' his client with a cup of tea, drawn from a tin vessel kept simmering over a kerosene flame on the counter. John is now at leisure to follow his bent for gambling and he wends his way to the gambling dens, which are conveniently close at hand. Here all the fire and energy of John's nature are brought out. In other pursuits he is one of those steady plodding creatures, but if winning at

The main street of Lawrence's Chinatown, 1904. Note weather-boarded buildings and (on right) the Joss House, with fixed ladder and lamp outside.
Otago Witness, 1904

Front view of Joss House. Note Chinese panelling.
Otago Witness, 1904

Interior of a Chinese gaming house in New Zealand.
Illustrated Press

The Joss House rebuilt as a holiday cottage in Lawrence.

The Chinese Empire Hotel, rebuilt in brick in 1884 by Sam Chew Lain, still stands beside today's main highway.

gambling he gets well nigh frantic with delight. If he loses he will seek solace in the opium den which is boxed in behind the gambling den. Here the disappointed gamblers puff away in sullen silence, until the foetid atmosphere around them becomes a dead weight under which they drop back into a state of semi-consciousness."

In 1869 a Joss House (public hall) was opened in the township with Europeans being invited to the ceremony. "The religious rites included roast pork, porter and fire crackers and were joined in with great fervour by many Europeans as well as Chinamen. The erection of the Joss House here will prove highly beneficial to the community as here it will now be possible to administer an oath to Chinese emigrants." Fortuitously this important Joss House was saved by the foresight of a university woman who had it moved into Lawrence, where it survives today as a charming little holiday cottage.

In 1884 Sam Chew Lain rebuilt the original wooden Chinese Empire Hotel in solid brick. The hotel, which dominates all other buildings in early photographs of the township, survived the fire which swept

Sam Chew Lain's tomb in Lawrence cemetery.

highway from Lawrence. His massive tomb is quite a feature of the Lawrence cemetery.

The last resident of Lawrence's Chinatown was Chow Shim who died in 1945, a nonagenarian. In 2004 Dr James Ng, the authority on Chinese settlement in New Zealand, compiled a concept plan[11] for Lawrence's nationally important Chinatown, with a view to excavating the site and reconstructing this unique town. Archaeologists began excavating the site in March 2005.

Waipori

The first discovery of gold in the Waipori River basin was made by a party of miners on their way to Gabriels Gully. O'Hara and his

Below: Poppet head of the Otago Pioneer Quartz (OPQ) mine, the first quartz crushing battery in Otago. *Hocken Library*

through the town in 1898, its flagpole defiantly flying the Chinese Imperial dragon flag. Sam Chew Lain was well respected in Lawrence for his good conduct of the hotel, which still stands right beside the main

Right: Grooved guide board for five stamper rods of the OPQ battery, 1979, now rotted away. Battery foundations in background.

Remains of the "Victory wheel" in the OPQ reserve in 1979.

mates had taken a shortcut across the Lammerlaws and as they crossed the Verterburn branch of the Waipori River they thought it looked a likely place to prospect. They were right and when they arrived at Gabriels Gully they had 34 ounces of gold to show for it. This was December 1861, only six months after Gabriel Read's discovery, and no one seemed greatly interested.

For the first few years there were only 200-300 men working the Waipori River and its tributaries on the cold snowy uplands of the Lammerlaws. Then Davies discovered a nugget of 27 ounces, the largest nugget ever found in the whole Tuapeka goldfield, and the Waipori rush really took off, reaching a peak of about 1,000 in 1865.

In 1865 four Shetlanders discovered the Shetland reef, in a gully on the south side of the present Lake Mahinerangi. At first they broke the quartz down with picks and washed it in a cradle. Then they erected a quartz crushing battery with ten stampers to crush the quartz. This was the first quartz crushing battery in Otago and as such it was called the Otago Pioneer Quartz (OPQ) battery. The OPQ battery worked intermittently for many years until 1901, averaging one ounce of gold per ton of quartz crushed[1]. After that the battery was removed to Macetown, where it was rebuilt as the Homeward Bound battery.

Today, the foundations of the OPQ battery[10] can be seen about halfway up the gully in the OPQ reserve. At the head of the gully are the remains of the Cosmopolitan mine and in the bog at the foot of the gully are some relics of the Victory battery, including its large water wheel, the "Victory wheel".

Chinese miners outside their sod hut in China Gully, Waipori. Rev. Alexander Don on right.
Alexander Turnbull Library

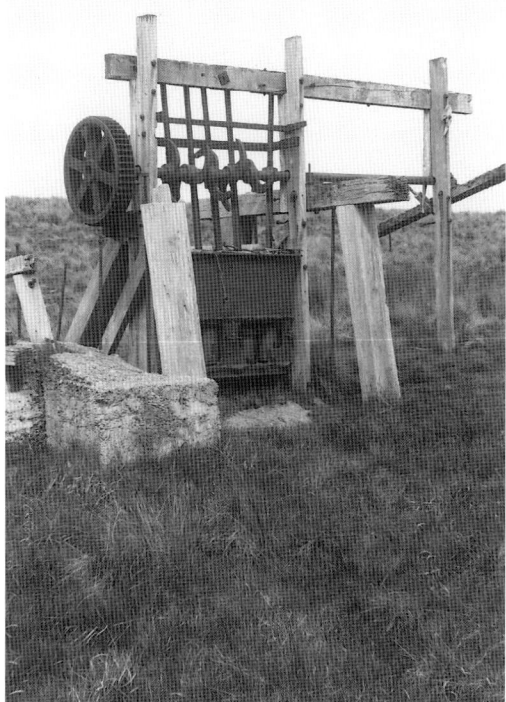

The Canton battery (in 1979), which is now collapsing sideways.

The wooden water wheel of the Canton battery (in 1979), which has now rotted away.

The Canton battery

In 1876 a Chinese party discovered the Canton quartz reef, near the foot of the OPQ Gully on Mitchells Flat. The Canton Company[9] was formed with an initial capital of 2,500 pounds, with one pound shares which were subscribed to by 2,000 Chinese scattered throughout New Zealand. A Chinese manager with considerable experience in Australia was engaged and plans were laid to sink a mine shaft, cut in water races and erect a crushing battery, the Canton battery. Although the mine was called the Canton, to the Chinese proprietors it was known as Lee Yuk, the Beneficial.[9]

Unfortunately the ground on which the Chinese were sinking their shaft was boggy and after becoming waterlogged they abandoned the mine. In 1889 it was taken over by Europeans. A most unusual sequence, as Chinese miners usually took over old European diggings on the goldfields.

Today the little Canton battery with its four stampers is the focus of attention in the OPQ reserve. Sadly its fine wooden water wheel has now rotted away and collapsed. The impressive system of water races that were dug to drive the various batteries in the OPQ reserve are preserved in the adjacent Pioneer Stream Reserve.

A drowned town

A sketch by A. H. Dunstan from a photograph in 1906 shows the arched bridge that once spanned the Waipori River at Waipori township. Across the bridge is the prominent two-storeyed Bridge Hotel and the various shops and stores that once lined the main street of the town, Flodden Street. Robert Cotton, a prominent farmer in the area, owned Cotton's store, next to the Bridge Hotel. William Knight's bakery was also in Flodden Street. There was also a Chinese store, owned by Kwong Wye Kee, to serve the large Chinese population of 450 on the goldfield.

> "The celebration of the Chinese New Year was a happy event shared by everyone. The chief attraction was a pole festooned with Chinese lanterns and a fireworks set called the 'ship' mounted on top. Purchasers of crackers at Kwong's store competed with each other in throwing lit crackers at the top of the pole. The first to light the ship received a prize."[1]

Interestingly Dunstan's sketch also shows a

Sketch from a photograph of Waipori township in 1906, showing the arched bridge across Waipori River and the huge *Waipori* dredge working at the edge of the town. *Hocken Library*

Left: Rev. George McNeur standing under the verandah of Kwong Wye Kee's corrugated iron store at Waipori, 1900. Chinese storekeeper on far left.
Alexander Turnbull Library

huge dredge, the *Upper Waipori,* almost 'threatening' the tiny town. The dredge was just one of sixteen which worked the Waipori River and its flats.

With the damming of the Waipori River in 1924 both the town and the main Waipori diggings on the river flats were drowned by Lake Mahinerangi. The Waipori cemetery survives on the northern hillside overlooking the drowned town.

The Maungatua robberies

In October 1861, fifteen travellers were waylaid, singly, or in twos or threes, at the foot of the Maungatua Hill on their way to Waipori and Gabriels Gully, relieved of their money and tied to trees. The leader of the Maungatua gang of robbers was Henry Garrett, a tall powerfully built man, recently arrived from Australia. Only two of the gang were arrested for the robberies. Anderson,

The Taieri Plain at the foot of Maungatua Hill where the Maungatua robberies took place. Painting by J. T. Thomson. *Hall-Jones family*

Right: Three of the Maungatua robbers who were later hanged in Nelson for murders on the West Coast and Nelson. From left: Burgess, Levy and Kelly. *P. May*

who received three years' imprisonment and Garrett, who was caught in Sydney and sentenced in Dunedin for eight years in prison. Two others, Thomas Kelly and Richard Burgess, later camped at Weatherstons. When surprised by the police in 1862 they fled to the hills, where they were captured by Sergeant-Major Bracken and Sergeant Trembill. Charged with shooting at Trembill, they were sentenced to three years' imprisonment. Another member of the gang, Philip Levy, later turned up at the German Hill diggings. All three of the last named were eventually hanged in Nelson 1866, after the grizzly Maungatapu murders in that province.

REFERENCES.
1. Mayhew, W. R., *Tuapeka*, 1949
2. Murray, J. S., *A Circulet of Gold*, 1984
3. Pyke, Vincent, *Early Gold Discoveries*, 1887
4. Hall-Jones, John, *John Turnbull Thomson*, 1992
5. John Cargill, son of Captain William Cargill.
6. Fulton, R. V., *Medical Practice in Otago in the Early Days*, 1922
7. Higham, C. and Vincent, B., *Gabriels Gully*. An Archaeological Survey, 1980.
8. Lemon, Daphne, *The Stars of Orion*, 1979
9. Ng, J., *Windows on a Chinese Past*, 1995
10. Easdale, S. and Jacomb, C., *Archaeology of the OPQ and Pioneer Stream Reserves*.
11. Ng, J., *Lawrence Chinese Camp Concept Plan*, 2004

CHAPTER 3
The Dunstan Rush

*Our object was to work only the richest spots
as we did not know how soon we might be discovered and rushed.*
Hartley and Reilly, August 1862

87 POUNDS WEIGHT of GOLD! So ran the headlines, large and bold, in the *Otago Daily Times* on 16 August 1862.

"Yesterday afternoon two men went to the Treasury, Dunedin, and deposited a bag of gold weighing eighty-seven pounds. They declined to say where they had obtained this rich parcel, but stated there was room for plenty more men where they had been working . . . Although the owners refused to state where they had obtained their gold we believe there is no doubt that it is from the neighbourhood of Mount Watkins, near Waikouaiti."

The fabulous weight of the gold, 87 pounds (1,044 ounces) was correct, but in reporting the source as Mt Watkins, Waikouaiti, the newspaper was widely out, north up the coast instead of 160 kilometres inland.

The basis of this wild guess was purely on the grounds that two strange men had been spotted stocking up with supplies at Waikouaiti.

The names of the two miners were Horatio Hartley and Christopher Reilly, both from California. When first interviewed by Vincent Pyke it soon became obvious that the two Californians were not prepared to reveal the source of their rich strike until a substantial reward was forthcoming. The experienced Pyke cast his eyes over the gold bag observing that[1] "a few small flakes had fallen out through the badly stitched seams into the tray on which the bag was placed. They were thin, warn and scaly, and I at once came to the conclusion that they had been subjected to the prolonged action of water amongst pebbles and boulders." With these observations Pyke concluded that the gold had been found in the vicinity of Lake Wanaka or the upper Clutha River, certainly not Mt Watkins.

"Hartley was very cool and circumspect during this interview, but Reilly was in a very excited state. I remember that in the course of conversation I incidentally remarked, by way of testing the accuracy of my notion as to the locality, 'The place where you got that gold was not far from Lake Wanaka'! Immediately Reilly jumped up, and cried out – 'Oh! We didn't come here to have our brains sucked. Come away, Hartley. And he made for the door. Hartley got up, but hesitated. 'Sit down, Mr. Hartley,'

Vincent Pyke, Secretary of the Otago Goldfields, who interviewed Hartley and Reilly when they brought their 87 pound bag of gold to him in August 1862.
Alexandra Museum

Hartleys Beach, 1899, with the *Hartley and Riley* [sic] dredge working off the beach. *Alexandra Museum*

said I; 'I have no desire to suck your brains; but Mr Reilly's conduct convinces me that I am right, and if you go out of this room before the agreement is signed, I will go straight to the place where you got the gold and you shall never have one penny of the reward.' Hartley sat down again silently; so did Reilly, and the business was quickly concluded."[1]

With the promise of a reward of 2,000 pounds, Hartley and Reilly described the location of their discovery as in the great gorge (the Dunstan Gorge, now Lake Dunstan) where the Clutha River cuts through the Dunstan Mountains (named by J. T. Thomson after Dunstanburgh Castle, during his survey in 1857).

On 19 August the *Otago Daily Times* released their interview with the two prospectors, getting the locality right this time.

"About twelve or fifteen miles below the junction of the Manuherikia we first obtained payable prospects. We tried a number of small bars that we thought would pay about an ounce a-day by working with a cradle. The river was very high at the time, and but little of the bars being out of water, we could not tell much about it. There are, however, for ten or fifteen miles below where we obtained our prospects, flats, and what appeared to be old channels of the river. We attempted to prospect several of them, but having no bucket or rope, and besides having the misfortune to break our shovel so as to render it valueless for sinking, we were not able to bottom, and were obliged to push on. The rich part of the river where we obtained the gold is between the Manuherikia and Upper Clutha Valleys. By the time we arrived here our provisions were exhausted, and our tin dish broken by a fall on the hillside, so that we could only wash a few handfuls of dirt at a time. We bought a little flour and borrowed a tin dish from one of the stations in the Manuherikia Valley, and panned out forty ounces in a week. We then went up the river as far as the junction of the Kawarau, and having satisfied ourselves that there was plenty more gold to be had, we started for Dunedin to get pack-horses and an outfit for a winter campaign. We returned by way of Waikouaiti and the Shag Valley. We did no cross the river at the old place, as we wished to avoid the people at the station who had seen us before. Our object was to work only the richest spots, as we did not know how soon we might be discovered and 'rushed'. For the first month or six weeks we were well satisfied with two or three ounces a day each, but as the river became lower and we learned more of the nature and extent of the diggings, we did not wash anything unless we thought it would pay about a pound weight a-day – that is six ounces each. The best dirt we found was the surface dirt on the bars. We did not usually wash more than from three to six inches of the top

Golden reflections in Lake Dunstan, which now covers Hartleys Beach.

BEGINNING OF DUNSTAN GOLDFIELD · 1862

"OUR OBJECT WAS TO WORK ONLY THE RICHEST SPOTS, AS WE DID NOT KNOW HOW SOON WE MIGHT BE DISCOVERED AND 'RUSHED'... WE DID NOT WASH ANYTHING UNLESS WE THOUGHT IT WOULD PAY ABOUT A POUND WEIGHT A DAY – THAT IS SIX OUNCES EACH..."

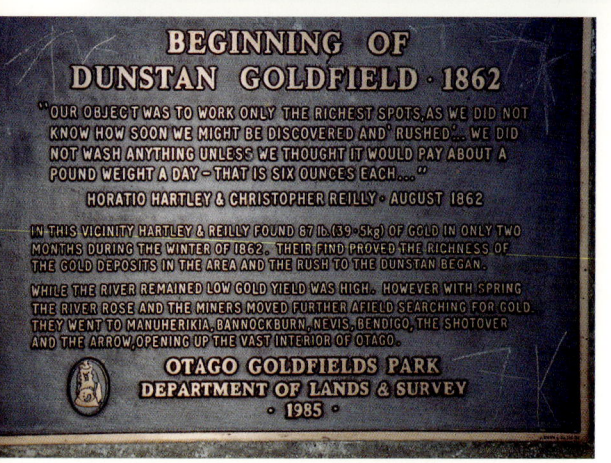

HORATIO HARTLEY & CHRISTOPHER REILLY · AUGUST 1862

IN THIS VICINITY HARTLEY & REILLY FOUND 87 lb. (39-5kg) OF GOLD IN ONLY TWO MONTHS DURING THE WINTER OF 1862. THEIR FIND PROVED THE RICHNESS OF THE GOLD DEPOSITS IN THE AREA AND THE RUSH TO THE DUNSTAN BEGAN.

WHILE THE RIVER REMAINED LOW GOLD YIELD WAS HIGH. HOWEVER WITH SPRING THE RIVER ROSE AND THE MINERS MOVED FURTHER AFIELD SEARCHING FOR GOLD. THEY WENT TO MANUHERIKIA, BANNOCKBURN, NEVIS, BENDIGO, THE SHOTOVER AND THE ARROW, OPENING UP THE VAST INTERIOR OF OTAGO.

OTAGO GOLDFIELDS PARK DEPARTMENT OF LANDS & SURVEY · 1985 ·

Roadside plaque, just south of Cromwell, commemorating Hartley and Reilly's famous discovery in 1862.

dirt – a loose sandy gravel easily washed – but in some places we took from one or two feet of it. We had nothing to do but to set the cradle at the edge of the river, and keep it going from morning till night, as one could get dirt and feed the cradle as fast the other could wash it. The gold is very fine, and accompanied by a great quantity of black sand. The gold we got on the bed rock is heavier, but we did not work any scarcely after the first month or so, as we found that we could not expect to make more than one to four ounces a-day, although we did find several good crevices, from one of which we took over twelve ounces in a few hours."[1]

It was an amazing story which evinced the spirit and determination of the true prospector. In the same way as Gabriel Read had set out to Tuapeka equipped with only a "spade, tin dish and butcher's knife", so had Hartley and Reilly gone forth with a "tin dish and shovel". Later, with their shovel and dish broken, they continued on prospecting with the aid of their hands. Clarifying their major discoveries in the Dunstan Gorge, Vincent Pyke records[1] how they first prospected "the western bank of the river and it was under the lofty rocks about two miles from the Kawarau [junction, later the site of Cromwell] that they made their first [big] find. This they named 'Reilly's Beach'."

"Further up the river they observed on the eastern bank [they had crossed over the Clutha River] a series of long rocky bars projecting into the stream, about a quarter of a mile below the junction of the Kawarau, and immediately beneath the site of the present Cromwell brewery [now Brewery Creek, below Cromwell]. Their Californian experience taught them that these bars, acting as natural 'ripples', afforded promise of yet better yields, and that in their clefts the richest deposits would be found. This place was subsequently named 'Hartley's Beach' [now marked with an historic plaque on the roadside south of Cromwell]."

"Retracing their steps they crossed the river at Fraser's station [William Fraser's Earnscleugh Station]. To avoid any wandering prospectors from Tuapeka, they went up the Manuherikia Valley and across the ranges to Waikouaiti, where they obtained supplies and returned by nearly the same route. It was this circumstance that gave rise to the impression that the new field was in the neighbourhood of Mt Watkins, past which the first part of their road lay. When they got back to the river 'Hartley's Beach' became the scene of their labours and it was there that they obtained the bulk of their famous 'Bag of Gold'."[1]

Deservedly Hartley and Reilly received the reward of 2,000 pounds for their discovery of a rich new goldfield, the Dunstan goldfield as it became known. They were just in time. For on the very day that they were dumping their 87 pound bag of gold on the counter of Dunedin's gold receiver, another party, Henry Stebbing's, was struggling down the gorges of the Clutha River to report their own discovery of gold in the Clutha, downriver from Dunstan Gorge. Stebbing's party had 'rediscovered' the gold at the junction of the Clutha and Manuherikia Rivers, as previously reported by Alexander Garvie. Unfortunately for Stebbing, he was three days late in applying for the bonus for discovering a new goldfield. But by way of consolation he was granted a substantial claim at the site of his discovery. Prospectors Point, on the south side of the junction, opposite the future town of Manuherikia (later renamed Alexandra).

The rush to Dunstan

The miners at Gabriels Gully learned about Hartley and Reilly's sensational 87 POUNDS of GOLD when Cobb & Co's coach arrived that same evening with copies of the *Otago Daily Times*.[1] Within an hour the whole diggings was astir. The startling news was read from the vantage of a barrel or dray, with the assistance of a bottle lantern, to attentive audiences. Within no time hundreds had made up their minds to try these fresh fields.

From the site of Alexandra looking across at the Clutha River flowing down the Roxburgh Gorge, the Manuherikia River entering from the left. Prospectors Point, where Henry Stebbing's party discovered gold, on the left.

84

The Dunstan Rush

Facing page, above: From the end of the Knobby Range looking down on the 'tent town' of Alexandra at the junction of the Clutha River and Manuherikia River (entering from the right). Track leading across the open plain to Dunstan (Clyde) at the entrance of the Dunstan Gorge in the Dunstan Mts. Sketch by Patrick Lysaght in December 1862. *Alexander Turnbull Library*

Facing page, below: Similar view by Frank Nairn in 1863, showing the ferry on the Manuherikia waterfront at Alexandra and a more obvious Dunstan (Clyde) at the entrance to the Dunstan Gorge. *Alexander Turnbull Library*

They had a two day start on their 'cousins' in Dunedin and were determined to get there first. Some even set out that evening. But just where "The Dunstan" was nobody really knew. All they had to go on was that it was "a gorge where the Clutha cuts through the Dunstan Mountains". No thought was given to there being not a single store in the whole wide area, only half a dozen sheep stations, where hopefully they could purchase meat. They just wanted to get there first and stake out their claims.

By the morning of 19 August Gabriels Gully and Weatherstons were virtually deserted. From Evans Flat they followed the runholders' track which climbed the steep "Big Hill" (now the line of the main highway) and descended to the Beaumont River and Beaumont station. Staying on the east side of the Clutha River they passed through the big Teviot station (owned by John Cargill, a son of Captain Cargill) and crossed the Teviot River at its mouth (now the site of East Roxburgh). They then ascended the Knobby Range (over 1,000 metres high) to at last obtain a view of their 'El Dorado'. An early artist, Patrick Lysaght, captures the scene in a sketch (in late December 1862) looking down on the 'tent

A closer view of Dunstan (Clyde) at the entrance to the Dunstan Gorge, 1870. Tracks leading down to the miners' huts, dangerously close to the flood-prone Clutha River. *Alexandra Museum*

town' of "Lower Dunstan" (Alexandra) forming at the junction of the Manuherikia and Clutha Rivers. From there a track leads across the open plain to a similar township, "Upper Dunstan" (Clyde), at the entrance to the fabled Dunstan Gorge in the Dunstan Mountains.

From this superb lookout the prospectors descended steeply to the Manuherikia River, where a ferry was soon installed and so across the plain to the Dunstan Gorge.

Meantime, for those would-be 'fortune seekers' heading from Dunedin the most popular and easiest route to "The Dunstan" was by way of Shag Valley and across the Maniototo Plain. But there was still no road north of Dunedin, so the trek began by steamer to Waikouaiti, where Johnny Jones' store did a roaring trade outfitting men with gear and food.

But the Shag Valley route was a long way round, so hardier types took a shortcut, the "mountain track", across the Rock and Pillar Range. Over 1,000 metres high it was subject to snow storms and was a dangerous place to be caught in the winter months. Later the "mountain track" was developed as the Dunstan Road for wagons and coaches.

The eager gold seekers streamed in from all three routes, Gabriels Gully, the "mountain track" and Shag Valley to converge on the Dunstan Gorge, where a 'canvas town', "The Dunstan" (Clyde), sprang up. Continuing up the steep craggy gorge they encountered Hartley at his famous Hartleys Beach. A kilometre beyond the beach, at the outlet of the gorge, was the junction of the Clutha and Kawarau Rivers, where another township, "The Junction" (later named Cromwell), quickly formed.

A few days after the start of the rush Captain Jackson Keddell accompanied Horatio Hartley back to the Dunstan Gorge. As officer commanding the gold escort, he had been made Commissioner of the new Dunstan goldfield to register the miners' claims. Arriving at Hartleys Beach they were met by hundreds of disgruntled miners. Many were 'new chums' to the game and those that came from Gabriels Gully could see no flat ground for digging. All they could see was a precipitous boulder-strewn gorge and a swiftly flowing river. Where were they supposed to start digging? There were mutterings towards Hartley of "throw him in the river" and "give him fifty lashes". Backed by Keddell and his escort, the taciturn Californian patiently explained to the angry assemblage that here the gold was trapped in the rock bars out in the river. Then calmly taking a pan he stepped out into the river and (luckily) was able to demonstrate to the astonished crowd that there was ample gold to be had. Seizing his opportunity, Keddell explained that all miner's claims had to be properly registered through him. Within a few days every metre of the river beaches had been taken up from Cromwell right down to Alexandra and into the Roxburgh Gorge beyond. Towards the end of 1862 upwards of 70,000 ounces[1] of

Gold escort at Clyde c.1870. *Alexandra Museum*

The Dunstan Rush

gold had been brought out from the Dunstan goldfield under escort to Dunedin. A considerable amount was also taken out by private hand.

THE GREAT FLOOD OF 1862

It began in September 1862 when warm north-west winds melted the snow in the mountains of the back country. The rivers rose with surprising speed, flooding all the beach claims. Many miners were caught unawares and their tents and gear were swept away in the swollen, swirling river.

Driven from their claims the miners took to the hills and prospected the gullies of the surrounding ranges. Reports of rich discoveries came pouring in. One of the first and most productive findings was at Conroys Gully. Close by were Butchers Gully, Obelisk Creek (now Fruitlands) and the Fraser River. High on the Old Man Range were Campbells Creek and Potters.

Conroys Gully

Thanks to the researches of Professor John McCraw[2] we now have a clearer picture of the discovery of the rich gold in Conroys Gully, near Alexandra.

On 1 October 1862 (Henry?) Conroy sank a number of shafts in the middle basin (now Dawsons Flat) of Conroys Gully to obtain 16 pennyweights of gold in 16 washes of his pan. He reported his discovery to Commissioner Keddell at Dunstan (Clyde), who returned with Conroy to inspect the site of the new discovery. Following up Conroys Creek from where it joins the Fraser River at Alexandra, they skirted a rocky chasm to arrive at Dawsons Flat, already a busy scene of activity with a 100 or so miners working the new field.

By the end of October fantastic returns were being reported by those miners fortunate enough to be 'on the gold', the narrow line of an old buried bed of Conroys Creek. One miner and his mate washed out 60 ounces of gold in eight days,[2] another party of four returned 9 pounds of gold in three weeks, while another two were said to have recovered 50 pounds of gold. So rich was the ground that the miners no longer talked in pennyweights (1/20th of an ounce) and ounces, but pounds of gold per week!

Restored Chinese rock shelter in Conroys Gully

Below: Schist-slab bed inside the shelter.

C. Field's Butchers Gully Hotel and general store, 1880s. Cobb & Co's coach outside.
Alexander Turnbull Library

Right: Butchers Dam and reservoir which flooded the township and diggings at Butchers Gully.

By November 1862, 400 miners had swarmed to Conroys Gully, but with such concentrated activity in the narrow confines of the gully newcomers had to spread out from the middle basin (Dawsons Flat) to the lower and upper basins (the latter now largely submerged by Conroys Dam).

By the 1870s, when most of the Europeans had moved away, Chinese miners moved in and reworked Conroys Gully, particularly the upper basin and Aldinga Creek, a tributary of upper Conroys Creek. John McCraw mentions[2] the unverified report of a 12 ounce nugget recovered by the Chinese in Conroys Gully, the largest found so far in the district.

In 1871 a five stamper crushing battery was erected in the chasm in the lower Conroys Gully to work a quartz reef which had been discovered there. But the returns were poor and the battery was sold the following year. Later two other batteries were erected in the chasm, but were equally unsuccessful.

Photograph by George Chance of Lye Bow's cottage at Butchers Dam. The cottage is still there.
Alexandra Museum

Today, in the DOC Aldinga reserve above Conroys Dam are the remains of the miners' water races, sluicings, tailings and some rock shelters, most of which are Chinese. One particularly interesting Chinese rock shelter, beneath an overhanging bluff, was restored for the film, *Illustrious Energy*. Inside is a solid stone bed made of schist slabs. At Dawsons Flat, the miner turned orchardist, Richard Dawson, reclaimed the miners' diggings to cultivate the now famous Dawson's cherries.

Butchers Gully

During the same month, October 1862, gold was discovered in Butchers Gully, adjacent to Conroys Gully. But the gold in Butchers Gully was not as rich as at Conroys. Notwithstanding, by 1863 there were 150 miners working in Butchers Gully and in 1865 Charles Nieper and Henry Wilkinson erected a butchery and store there, the latter also serving as an illegal grog shop, a common practice in those days.

Later the Butchers Gully Hotel was built at the gully, but after this was destroyed by fire in 1886 a replacement hotel was constructed in stone.

With the construction of the Butchers Dam in 1937, the hotel and most of the diggings were flooded by the reservoir. Nevertheless some remains of the sluicings can be seen on the new DOC Flat Top Hill walkway.

Closely associated with Butchers Gully were the market garden and orchard of Lye Bow, a Chinese ex-miner. A popular figure in the district, old timers used to recall the potency of his peach brandy. The remains of Lye Bow's cottage, orchard and garden still exist among the trees at the head of the reservoir.

Bald Hill Flat (Fruitlands)

Descending parallel to Butchers and Conroys Creeks from the Old Man Range, Obelisk Creek debouches onto Bald Hill Flat (now Fruitlands) on today's highway to Queenstown.

Although the discovery of gold in Obelisk Creek was later than Butchers and Conroys Creeks, by 1 August 1863 there was a rush to Bald Hill Flat, where Andrew Drew[4] and Ben Buchanan were getting an ounce of gold in 30 buckets from a depth of only one foot below the surface. Over the next few years the whole of Bald Hill Flat was prospected, with small amounts of gold recovered from shallow depths almost everywhere.

Bald Hill Flat was an outlying part of John Cargill's vast Teviot station and after negotiations with Cargill and Edward Anderson (the co-owner) Bald Hill Flat was split off the Teviot run and subdivided into sections for lease. Probably the first miner to take up a section was John Kemp who built the Cape Broom Hotel and store in stone on

John Kemp's original Cape Broom Hotel at Bald Hill (Fruitlands) with the owner and his sister outside, c.1870. *Alexandra Museum*

Left: Hexagonal dairy of Cape Broom Hotel, 2005

his section. Later, when he was able to freehold his section he built a much larger two-storeyed Cape Broom Hotel. The hotel was not named after Cape Broome in Australia, as so many people think, but the 'Cape Broom' plant which Kemp used as a hedge to subdivide his garden. In 1910 John Kemp's second Cape Broom Hotel was burnt down, but the stone shell remains, also an attractive hexagonal dairy alongside.

Water for sluicing and later elevating was the key to the continuation of mining at Bald Hill Flat. Water races were cut from as far afield as Shingle Creek (near Roxburgh) and a 'bracket' of races was brought in from Gorge Creek. Prominent among the race-makers were the Mitchell brothers from Shetland, Andrew and John, who also constructed a holding dam, Mitchells Dam, behind the now historic John Mitchell's stone cottage. While ground-sluicing was in vogue the need for water was comparatively low, but with the introduction of hydraulic elevators the demand rocketed, resulting in a spate of race construction. After the phase of hydraulic elevators, a large dredge was built on Bald Hill Flat, just below John Kemp's Cape Broom Hotel. It started dredging in March 1901, but proved an abysmal failure and ceased operations only three months later.[4]

High above Bald Hill Flat, on a ridge leading up to the great Obelisk of the Old Man Range, the cousins James White and Andrew Mitchell discovered a gold-bearing quartz reef in 1876.[4] Shortly after their discovery James White bought out Andrew

Sluice gun and hydraulic elevator working at Fruitlands. *Alexandra Museum*

Right: Andrew Mitchell's stone hut at White's reef, later the Vincent Ski Club hut.

Mitchell's share of their claim and formed a company, White's Reef Co, to purchase a quartz crushing battery. A five stamper battery was eventually erected in 1886 and for four years the company prospered, returning 1,000 ounces of gold per year. Then suddenly the gold ran out and the battery was purchased by the Symes brothers, Robert and Henry. As manager, Robert Symes rejuvenated the battery and mine and continued working by both sluicing and crushing until as late as 1927.

Today the road up to the Obelisk is rightly known as Symes Road. Below Symes Road, in the watershed of Obelisk Creek, is the stone hut originally built by Andrew Mitchell before it became White's Reef claim. Fortuitously the Vincent Ski Club took over the hut in the 1950s, renovating and preserving it by adding a new corrugated iron roof.

As for Bald Hill Flat, the name changed to the more euphonious one of Fruitlands in 1915, in recognition of it becoming a fruit growing area. Here are the remains of miners' stone cottages, some derelict, others restored, also some modern houses. The most famous of them all is the superbly crafted stone cottage of John Mitchell, who lived there with his wife, Jessie, and their ten children. The masterly stone masonry of the cottage is in keeping with the stone cottages in Shetland and extends to the outbuilding, stone walls, chicken coup and even the toilet. But the 'piece de resistance' is the sundial platform

John and Jessie Mitchell's stone cottage at Fruitlands.

Left: Jessie Mitchell who raised their ten children in the cottage. DOC

chipped from a solid block of schist. Uphill behind the cottage are the drilled rock tors where the Mitchell brothers obtained the schist blocks to build the cottage.

Campbells

With the rich deposits of gold in the gullies of Conroys, Butchers and Obelisk Creeks there must surely be a massive mother lode on the top of the Old Man Range, the miners reasoned. But the exposed snow-prone tops of the Old Man Range are a grim place to be caught in a snow storm, as the miners soon learned to their cost.

In early December 1862 the Campbell brothers, Alex[4] and John ("Little Johnny")[5] and party discovered gold in Campbells Creek high on the summit slopes of the Old Man Range. With good returns from the diggings at Campbells Creek, a little 'canvas' township of miners' tents and stores evolved at 'Campbells Gully'. But the ground available for mining was limited and the miners spread out to prospect the surrounding country. In a shallow, peaty basin at the head of a small stream (Potters No. 2) draining into Campbells Creek, John Lishman Potter discovered gold. Potter had previously found gold in the Nevis Valley (Potters No. 1), so his second discovery became known as Potters No. 2.

Other prospectors followed Campbells Creek down from their 'township' into a deep gorge where they discovered rich gold. But to mine the gorge they had to drive a tunnel (200 metres long)[4] through a slip below the gorge to act as a tail race to get rid of their tailings. As such the mine became known as the Tunnel claim. The Tunnel party also constructed a massive stone wall to divert Campbells Creek so that

Potters No. 2 on the open tops of the Old Man Range, the Garvie Mts beyond. John Bennetts' hut is the more distant of the two.

Drilled rock tors where the Mitchell brothers obtained the schist slabs to build the cottage.

Left centre: Miner's stone hut at the Tunnel claim, Campbells Creek, 1979.

Massive stone wall built to divert Campbells Creek, 1979.

they could work the stream bed. Although the tunnel has since become obliterated the massive stone wall and the remains of the miners' stone huts survive and serve as impressive reminders of the hardy miners of the Tunnel party.

The Tunnel claim continued operations, though seasonally, right up to 1900. In April 1894 one of the Tunnel claim miners George Dugan,[9] became lost when returning to the claim in a snow storm and collapsed within only 300 metres of his hut.

John Lishman Potter who discovered the gold at Potters No. 1 (in the Nevis) and Potters No. 2. *Peter Chandler*

Right: Inscribed headboard on the grave of William Pitt, an elderly miner who died of hypothermia when approaching Potters on 20 June 1864. Photographed in 1979, the headboard has now been replaced by a quartz headstone.

Potters No. 2

John Lishman Potter, the discoverer of the gold at Potters No. 2, was interviewed in 1927 by Gratton Grey:[5]

"Mr Potter, who is nearly 100 years old, is thought to be the only living survivor of the famous Eureka rebellion [at Ballarat in Australia]. He is still in possession of all his faculties and energy, and carries on his business of a builder and contractor in Timaru. Although his hair is now snow white, he is wonderfully preserved. He has never worn glasses, never lost a tooth, has never had a day's sickness and never feels tired. He neither drinks nor smokes and still retains a clear recollection of all events connected with the rising of the diggers at the battle of the Eureka stockade. He was the discoverer of three different goldfields [in New Zealand. The location of Potters No. 3 is obscure]."

Born in Sunderland, England in 1834, John Lishman Potter took part in the Eureka rebellion at Ballarat in 1854. In 1861 he followed the gold rush across to New Zealand to Gabriels Gully, later taking part in the anniversary celebrations in 1911 and 1921. After discovering Potters No. 2 he stayed on only briefly, moving to Timaru where he lived for many years carrying on business as a builder. He died in Timaru on 24 October 1931 aged 97.[6]

Potters No. 2 was not the sort of place to dwell in the winter time. The Reverend Alexander Don[7] visiting Potters in January 1892 saw three graves of goldminers who lost their lives in the winter of 1864. Two were unknown, but one was marked with "a board inscribed William Pitt, died 20 June 1864. At that time several snow poles were still standing on the track from Campbells, but only fragments of the connecting wire were lying about." (The "inscribed board" has been

The Dunstan Rush

Historian Peter Chandler standing amid the ruins of Andrew Ree's hut, 1979.

removed for safe-keeping at the Waikaia Museum and replaced by a white quartz headstone. One of the "unknown" graves noted by Don has recently been identified by E. J. Dwyer[9] as that of Nicholas Cordts, a German miner.)

John Bennetts' hut at Potters No. 2, 1979.

Left: Andrew Ree who worked at Potters No. 2 from 1873 to 1923. *Peter Chandler*

The last of the old diggers to leave Potters was Andrew Ree[5] (not Rees, as previously reported. Peter Chandler, a meticulous researcher, tracked down his death certificate, which clarifies this name). Andrew Ree lived in a substantial stone hut of two rooms, protected from the blizzards by a stone wing. He was well aware of death from exposure and took no chances. His peat shed, which was also built of stone, was only a couple of paces from the door of his house and he always left Potters in the autumn to spend the winter down country. In the autumn of

1923 Andrew Ree, after a lifetime of mining at Potters, closed the door of his hut for the last time and departed for Timaru where he died in 1926 aged 84. The ruins of his stone hut can still be seen at Potters.

The well preserved hut at Potters today belonged to John Bennetts,[5] a comparative newcomer, who constructed a water race at Potters in 1932.

The Great Snow of 1863

Thanks to John McCraw[4] we now know the location of the elusive Chamonix, the packers' village for supplying Campbells and Potters. John McCraw's researches show that Chamonix was is the deep gully of Gorge Creek at its junction with Hut Creek, well above the present main highway. With "about 20 stores, shanties, tents and a blacksmith's shop", it was a busy little service village. From Chamonix it was a stiff climb up Gorge Creek to the summit of the Old Man Range and perhaps with some premonition that a snowfall could bring disaster, the government marked the route with snow poles in the autumn of 1863.

In July 1863 the snow began to fall and the more prudent of the miners at Campbells and Potters moved down to Chamonix and Alexandra. Misguidedly, a large number, fearing that their claims might be 'jumped', elected to winter it out. With snow lying on the hills the packers were unable to get through and the miners began to run out of food. The crisis came on 11 August when very heavy snow storms began to sweep over the range. Fearing starvation the wintering miners decided to make a break for Chamonix. It was a fatal decision, they had left it too late.

On 18 August exhausted men began staggering into Chamonix with news of a disaster. Parties breaking out from Campbells had been caught in a blizzard. With whiteout conditions on a bleak, featureless mountainside, they wandered aimlessly till they collapsed and died of hypothermia.

The story of the sole survivor of a party of four miners was told to Warden H. W. Robinson at an inquiry conducted in Alexandra:[1]

> "One incident of very tragic interest was the case of a party of four men who started together for Alexandra. First one lost heart and soon he dropped behind. Then another could not keep up, and he had to be left by the other two. These two kept on manfully together until they also could proceed no further and took shelter from the storm behind a rock. The weaker of the two could not keep on his feet, and his friend lifted him up when he fell and propped him against the rock, trying all he could to keep the poor fellow from yielding to the drowsiness which he knew meant death. At last the faithful friend could keep him up no more. He sank down and the other had no strength left to rise him. Still the last man kept himself up – at length day dawned and the storm abated – and the solitary watcher by the dead saw that he was within a quarter of a mile of the shanty, where all could have been safe if only they could have seen and reached it.
>
> "The bodies of the three men were never brought down, but when the track was once more opened they were found and buried where they lay – (at least I believe such was the case). There was no inquest, but I held an informal magisterial inquiry at Alexandra. I remember I was greatly struck with the manly demeanour of the survivor whose statement I took down."

The number of miners who perished was greatly exaggerated in the newspapers, some giving the count as high as 50. This figure was reduced by Warden Robinson to 30, but as E. J. Dwyer points out in his meticulously researched *Deaths on the Old Man Range* (2003),[9] Robinson's figure included an unproven extra 17 given to him by an unreliable source. Dwyer[9] in his excellent survey concludes that a total of 12 miners, all of whom he tracks down and names, perished in the Great Snow of 1863. There may have been a thirteenth victim, the unidentified skeletal remains of a man found "near the

Remains of old wooden snow pole (in the centre of the stones) erected on the Old Man Range in 1863. Photographed in 1979.

Roadside monument at Gorge Creek erected in memory of the miners who perished in the Great Snow of 1863. Snow-flecked Old Man Range in background.

Painted schist headstone of John Stewart's grave, 130 metres below the Gorge Creek monument. There are three other unmarked, but known graves in the vicinity.

top of the Old Man Range in 1873".

In 1929 a roadside monument was erected at Gorge Creek to the miners who perished in the Great Snow of 1863, a stern reminder not to venture out to the open tops in winter conditions.

On a track 130 metres below the monument is a schist headstone with a red cross on it, which marks the grave of John Stewart, one of the victims of the Great Snow. John Stewart[10] was well known as a ferryman on the Clutha River, where he had a bullock-hide boat for crossing. But the lure of gold led him to seek a rapid fortune on the Old Man Range, only to perish in the snow storm. So highly did the local community regard Stewart that after the snow thawed, eighteen men climbed the range and carried his body down to Gorge Creek for burial.

There are three other graves around John Stewart's headstone, all fellow victims of the same storm, which Dwyer[9] has traced and has been able to name.

Fraser River Basin

The source of the Fraser River is in a large boggy basin on the other (western) side of the Old Man Range from Conroys Gully. In November 1862 gold was discovered in the Fraser River Basin and soon there were 200 miners working in this new field. At an altitude of 1,400 metres it was higher than Potters and Campbells. What with frozen snow lying deeply in the basin during the

The giant water wheel of the Alpine Reef battery in the headwaters of the Fraser River. *Alexandra Museum*

In 1968 the water wheel was dismantled and re-erected in Alexandra.

winter, it was a bitterly cold place to work. Fortuitously the miners learned to evacuate the basin before winter, avoiding the disaster of the Great Snow of Campbells and Potters in 1863.

In 1862 Charles Nicholson[4] of Ettrick formed a company, the Alpine Quartz Reef Co, to mine a supposed gold-bearing quartz reef that had been discovered right at the head of the Fraser Basin A ten stamper crushing battery was purchased and carted to the Alpine Quartz Reef claim, where it was erected with a large water wheel to drive it. But there the venture ended. There were no reports of quartz being crushed or gold being recovered. Doubtless the high altitude of the mine, preventing operations during the winter months, was one of the reasons why the battery was soon abandoned.

During 1968-70 the big water wheel was dismantled and transported to Alexandra, where it was re-erected outside the old museum. The remains of the battery lie in remote Battery Creek in the Fraser Basin.

Doctors Point

Who the doctor of Doctors Point was nobody seems to know. No medical

The Dunstan Rush

Remains of the 10 stamper Alpine Reef battery in 2003. Alexandra Museum

practitioner is known to have either worked at or visited the point, nor is any doctor's name associated with this goldfield. Maybe it was a miner who served as a 'dentist' when his fellow workers suffered from toothache. Or maybe it was the miners' term for visiting the 'doctor' (proprietor) at the local sly grog shop to obtain a bottle of 'painkiller'.

Whatever the explanation, in 1864 gold was discovered at Doctors Point, on the east side of the Clutha River about eight kilometres below Alexandra. Although nobody made his fortune at Doctors Point the field was worked for a very long period from 1864 until the 1930s. Water for sluicing was brought in by water race and pipeline from Shanty Creek and tail races were built with stone walls. Overhanging rocks were closed off with stone walls to create rock shelters, while other miners built stone huts. Many of these rock shelters in the Roxburgh Gorge were built by Chinese miners.

Most of the gold was high on the hillside above the river (before Lake Roxburgh was raised) indicating an older level of riverbed[2]

Restored rock shelter on the Doctors Point track.

and as such, huge 'river' boulders had to be removed to get at the goldfield. A massive water-powered winch, with a two-way system of Pelton wheels, was installed with a wire rope to drag the boulders off the field. This huge winch is one of the special features of

Restored rock shelter at Doctors Point. Once a hillside shelter, it is now a lakeside shelter on the edge of Lake Roxburgh.

Old Teviot River ford (just below the present Teviot bridge), where in 1862 Young and Woodhouse discovered the gold that triggered gold mining in the Roxburgh district.

tunnelling into the hillside. As a result we have one of the best examples of alluvial gold mining in the Otago goldfields, making the DOC walk (a full day) down the gorge to Doctors Point well worthwhile.

Teviot (East Roxburgh)

In 1862 Andrew Young and James Woodhouse were on their way from Gabriels Gully to the Dunstan rush with a couple of mates. Arriving at the Teviot River, Young offered to piggy-back the others across the ford. Safely across, the first two sped on their way, leaving Young and Woodhouse drying out their clothes. While they waited they filled in time with some tentative prospecting in the Teviot River. Their results were so good that they decided to stay put. As they pegged out their claims at the junction of the Teviot and Clutha Rivers they were soon joined by others rushing to The Dunstan. So began gold mining in the Roxburgh area. Today, a monument marks the site of the discovery at the ford, just below the present Teviot Bridge.

Doctors Point and is to be found in the upper workings about 80 metres above Lake Roxburgh.

During the depression years of the 1930s some 80 miners lived in the gorge, repairing the water race for sluicing and also re-

Pinders Pond, Teviot, an old dredge pond, now a tree-girt swimming pool.

Right: Restored walking bridge across the Clutha River at Horseshoe Bend.

Both sides of the Clutha River were prospected at the junction, but the east bank proved to be the better and so evolved the township of Teviot (now East Roxburgh). Later, when the main Queenstown highway was constructed up the west side of the Clutha, the main (present) town of Roxburgh shifted over to the west side.

Horseshoe Bend Diggings

In 1863 three Irishmen discovered gold at the Horseshoe Bend[3] of the Clutha River, on

The "Lonely Graves" at Horseshoe Bend.

the east side, eight kilometres down from Millers Flat. Pegging off claims, they were soon rewarded with returns that were seldom less than an ounce a day. Their activities could hardly escape the notice of parties on their way to The Dunstan and soon there was a population of some 200-300[3] miners and storekeepers at the Horseshoe Bend diggings. By 1865 most had drifted on to other rushes further inland, leaving only 72 at the diggings.

The Horseshoe Bend diggings are probably best known by the popular legend about the "Lonely Graves". According to the story, in 1865 William Rigney found the body of a good-looking young man washed up on a beach at Horseshoe Bend. After the inquest into the death of the unknown young man, Rigney arranged for his burial and later marked the grave with a wooden headboard, "Somebody's Darling lies buried here". Without wishing to spoil a good story, it is now established that the 'unknown' man was a Charles Alms, a butcher from the Nevis Valley. In 1901 Rigney wrote a letter to the *Tuapeka Times* pointing out that he had neither found nor buried the body. Nevertheless, when Rigney died in 1912 he was buried beside "Somebody's Darling".

By 1900 the population of Horseshoe Bend had dwindled to about 30 and the main road had long since shifted to the other side of the river. For the children to get to school they had to row across the river by boat. In 1887 a wire cage was installed, but one end was higher than the other and the children had difficulty in pulling themselves 'uphill'. Eventually in 1913 a walking bridge was built across the river. This historic bridge was recently restored, with access walkways from either end.

REFERENCES
1. Pyke, Vincent, *Early Gold Discoveries in Otago*, 1887
2. McCraw, John, *Mountain Water and River Gold*, 2000.
3. Webster, A. H., *Teviot Tapestry*, 1948.
4. McCraw, John, *Gold on the Dunstan*, 2003
5. Hall-Jones, John, *Goldfields of the South*, 1982.
6. Chandler, Peter, *Glenaray*, 1984.
7. Don, Alexander, *Otago Daily Times*, November, 1882.
8. DOC brochure, *Mitchell's Cottage*.
9. Dwyer, E. J., *Deaths on the Old Man Range*, 2003
10. Gilkison, Robert, *Early Days in Central Otago*, 1930

CHAPTER 4
All Roads lead to Dunstan

*The horses climbed the steep hillside road,
heads down and panting heavily,
while the passengers walked alongside.*
The Dunstan Road, E. M. Lovell-Smith

With the hordes of hungry prospectors arriving at the goldfields, the need for roads for supplies became urgent. The challenging task of constructing these roads fell to Chief Surveyor Thomson in his dual role of Chief Engineer to the province.[1]

Construction of a main road north of Dunedin would be slow because there were high hills to traverse A road south of Dunedin would require a very long bridge across the Taieri River, a major work. The shortest and quickest route to the goldfields would be to

Roads to Dunstan (Clyde) in the 1860s. *Copyright, J. Hall-Jones*

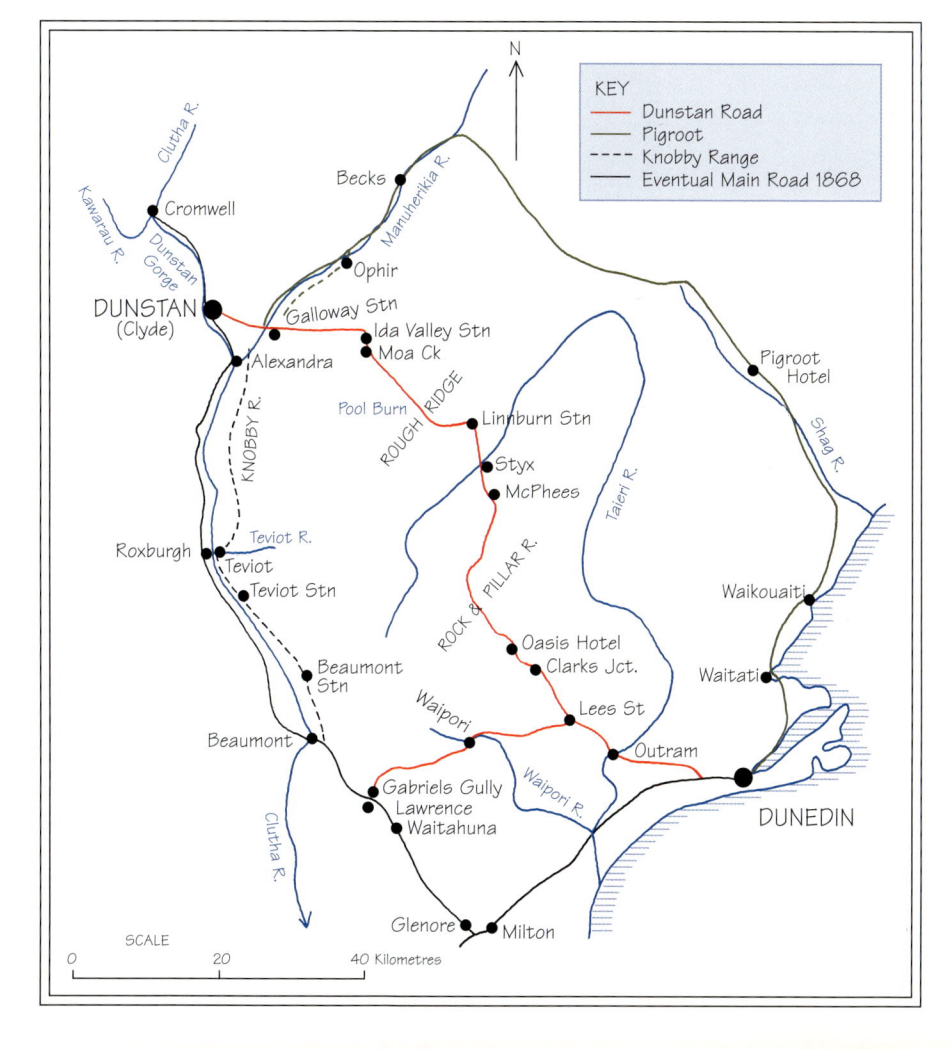

Thomson's bridge across the Taieri River at Outram, 1862. Painting by J. T. Thomson. *Hall-Jones family*

The old Lees Stream Hotel and Lees Stream bridge, 1979.

head directly west. A road that stuck to the tussocks and ridges, avoiding the bogs, would allow construction with the least amount of metalling and the minimum delay. Thomson knew the Lammerlaws and Rock and Pillar Range well, having surveyed and named both. His mind was made up, this was the way to go.

The Dunstan Road

The road began on the Taieri Plain, near Outram, where Donald Borrie ran a ferry across the Taieri River, until the Outram bridge was completed. Designed by Thomson and constructed in Oamaru stone it was completed in commendable time in 1862 and remained in full use right up till 1966. (The foundations can be seen upriver from the modern bridge.)

As the road ascended the Lammerlaw Hills a branch struck south to the Waipori diggings and Gabriels Gully. At Lees Stream (the correct spelling, as named by Thomson after Lees Stream on the Borders)[1] there was another stone bridge and the Lees Stream Hotel, owned by Diamond.[2] (The derelict

All Roads lead to Dunstan 59

remains of both structures are still there.) Near Clarks Junction, John Clark built the original Clarks Junction Hotel, on the site of the present one. The road continued on to Deep Stream, where the coach often stopped for dinner at John Kerry's tiny Oasis Hotel. At the Oasis Hotel "there was plenty of grog but no accommodation". So after dinner the coach continued up the steep Rock and Pillar Range, the horses "heads down and panting heavily, while the passengers walked alongside".[6] Out on the open tops were at least two more 'refreshment' stops, McDonald's big iron shanty[2] halfway across and further on "Mother" McPhee's grog shop and "Halfway House", at McPhee's Rock. A bleak and desolate spot, not the sort of place to get caught in a snowstorm. A passenger on Cobb & Co's coach, which first used the road in November 1862, describes McPhee's "Halfway House":[6]

"In the sitting-room, instead of the fire, there is a small stove, the size of a bread-baking tin. This Tom Thumb thing had to warm 50 passengers shivering from cold, and just arrived by the four coaches that evening. I had a meal seated on a brandy case, the chairs having all been taken. There were ten beds in one small room, and narrow stretchers at three shillings per night. On resuming our trip next day, there was not one single rood of level ground on the road to be seen. The driver chained the brake of the coach when going down several steep places. The weather was lovely but frosty, and we arrived at the Upper Taieri Ferry [Styx, now Paerau] with icicles hanging from the

The tiny Oasis Hotel (in 1970), where there was "plenty of grog but no accommodation".
June Wood

Left: The Dunstan Road climbing over the Rock and Pillar Range.

Below: The stables for the coach horses at Styx, 2005.

Below, at foot of page: The stalls and feed boxes inside.

The Styx gaol, 2004. Right: The shackles in the Styx gaol were used more for securing gold bullion than prisoners.

Dovecote in old historic farm building at Galloway station. Right: Sign on the old Moa Creek Hotel.

horses' bellies, while they steamed like a furnace. We had breakfast at this place."

There was usually an overnight stop at the Styx Hotel (recently rebuilt by a private owner). The gaol at Styx was more of a 'lock up' for the gold bullion than for criminals. From Styx the road took off across the Maniototo Plain to the Blackball Hotel (later used as a rabbiter's hut on Linnburn station). It then continued over Rough Ridge to Poolburn and the Ida Valley Station, where nearby was (and still is) the Moa Creek pub. Then skirting the Raggedy Range it passed through Galloway station before crossing the Manuherikia ford, at the end of the present Keddell Road. Then it was 'lickety-split' across the open plain to Dunstan (Clyde).

The Pigroot

The "mountain road" to Dunstan served its purpose. It was 50 kilometres shorter than the Shag Valley route (commonly known as the Pigroot) and it saved the double handling of a sea voyage to Waikouaiti and then a transfer to wagons or coaches But the steep climb over the Rock and Pillar Range was very hard on horses and it was impassable during the winter months because of snow.

To bypass the big hills north of Dunedin, Thomson had already surveyed and marked out (in 1858) a road over the lower slopes of Mt Cargill to Blueskin Bay (Waitati). So work on the Blueskin Bay Road could begin immediately. From Blueskin Bay the road

Snow-covered Dunstan Road at Poolburn Reservoir. *Below:* Ford across the Manuherikia River near Galloway Station.

Coach with horses in full gallop heading up the old Blueskin Road to Waitati. Painting by J. T. Thomson.
Juliet Hindmarsh

continued on to Waikouaiti and the start of the inland road up Shag Valley.

The Murison Brothers of Puketoi Station in the Maniototo had already pioneered a dray track up the Shag Valley in 1858, using a team of eight bullocks to draw their dray. A dramatic photograph of the Pigroot (as it soon became known) shows a convoy of horse-drawn wagons stopped at Brothers Hill in the Shag Valley, while a wheel is being dug out from the mud. Interestingly, in the background is Freeland's corrugated iron

Horse-drawn wagons stuck in the mud on the Pigroot, 1862. Freeland's Pigroot Hotel in the middle distance, Brothers Hill on the skyline. *Alexandra Museum*

White horse and coach at White Horse Hotel, Becks, 1892. *Alexandra Museum*

Horse-drawn wagons passing on Big Hill between Lawrence and Beaumont, 1902. *Alexandra Museum*

Pigroot 'Hotel', the 'halfway house' where passengers stopped for the night and horses were changed.

On reaching the Maniototo Plain the road took a long loop round Blackstone Hill (in line with the modern highway 85) before heading south to Black's station (Ophir) and Galloway Station, and so across the Manuherikia ford. Hotels sprang up all along the route, notably at Wedderburn, Blackstone Hill (Hills Creek), Becks (where the old hotel has been restored) and Ophir.

The Pigroot served a dual purpose, because by 1863 the Maniototo goldfields had been discovered. So branch roads were led off to the diggings at Naseby, Kyeburn, St Bathans, Hamiltons, Drybread, Tinkers and others (see Chapter 12).

From Gabriels Gully

There were two ways of reaching Gabriels Gully from Dunedin. One by ferry across the lower Taieri River, which was eventually replaced by a long bridge designed by Thomson. Then from Tokomairiro (Milton) the road headed inland via Glenore and Waitahuna to Gabriels Gully (along the line of the modern highway to Queenstown). The other was the branch off the Dunstan Road at Lees Stream and then across the bleak Lammerlaws to the Waipori River, which was crossed by a bridge, and so down to Weatherstons and Lawrence.

From Lawrence there was a steep grind up Big Hill and down to the Beaumont River, near its junction with the Clutha, where the township of Beaumont became established. Then, sticking to the east side of the Clutha River, the runholders' wagon track crossed the Beaumont River by a sapling bridge and began the steep, slippery climb up a narrow ridge, appropriately named the "Devil's Backbone",[3] to Beaumont station. The trail continued past John Cargill's Teviot station (where a huge woolshed, the largest in the country was built in 1880) and so on to the ford across the Teviot River (just below the present bridge), where Andrew Young and James Woodhouse had discovered the first gold in the Roxburgh area.

The huge stone woolshed at Teviot station, with its barrel-shaped ends and 40 shearing stands.
Pamela Hall-Jones

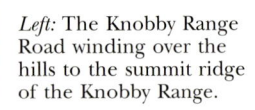

Left: The Knobby Range Road winding over the hills to the summit ridge of the Knobby Range.

Left: Deep wheel ruts carved in the schist on the long descent from the Knobby Range.

The Beaumont Ferry c.1880. *Burton Bros*

From the Teviot River crossing the road climbed steadily up the Knobby Range Road to the summit of the Knobby Range. The exposed summit ridge was over 1,000 metres high and subject to sudden snowstorms, so it was marked with a line of rock cairns, some of which still exist. At the end of the summit ridge instead of following the miners' steep walking track directly down to Alexandra, the coaches continued down a long leading ridge to the Manor Burn, their locked wheels grinding deep ruts in the soft schist all the way. The Manor Burn was crossed above the present lower dam and so across the Manuherikia River at Duncan Robertson's ford, 200 metres below the present Galloway bridge. (The ford was named after Duncan Robertson, who owned the Balmoral Hotel[5] there.)

Cobb & Co began their coach service on the Knobby Range Road in April 1865,[6] but the exposed summit ridge was often closed by snow during the winter months. It was a challenging route and it is said that only one driver, James Carmichael,[4] would take a coach across the Knobby Range Road. When the new main road to Dunstan was completed the high Knobby Range Road was abandoned for the low one.

A main road at last

By January 1863 the decision had been made. A main road (the route of the present Queenstown highway) would run from Milton to Lawrence, then on to Beaumont, where a ferry would carry traffic across the Clutha River until a bridge was built. From there the road would follow the west side of the Clutha up to the new Roxburgh township on the west bank, where a ferry would cross to Teviot (East Roxburgh), until there was a bridge. After the Teviot ferry, the road would continue temporarily over the Knobby Range until the new western road was completed.

By the end of 1864 the ferries were installed at Beaumont and Teviot. Work began on the new low road from Roxburgh to Alexandra up the west side of the Clutha in 1866 and was completed by 1868, with a large ferry across the Clutha to Alexandra.

The ferry at Teviot (East Roxburgh), with the definitive town of Roxburgh forming on the west bank of the Clutha River. Sketch by Andrew Hamilton, 1869. *Hamilton's sketchbook*

A similar view about the same time. Teviot in foreground, definitive town of Roxburgh on the far (west) bank with the ferry below. Painted by Ned Hughes, a miner at Roxburgh. *Otago Settlers Museum*

These journeys by coach were not without their hazards. The visiting English author, Anthony Trollope, recounts how they were caught in a snowstorm on Big Hill near Beaumont. The passengers disembarked to assist in shovelling the snow off the road. Although the famous author worked away with a will he concluded that he was "more at home with a pen than a shovel"! On another occasion the brake failed as the coach descended the steep Big Hill. A woman screamed. The horses bolted and the coach capsized. The horses broke away, colliding with a wagon team labouring up the hill.[6]

REFERENCES
1. Hall-Jones, John, *John Turnbull Thomson*, 1992.
2. Wood, June, *Gold Trails of Otago*, 1970
3. McCraw, John, *The Golden Junction*, 1992.
4. Webster, A. H., *Teviot Tapestry*, 1948
5. McCraw, John, *Gold in the Dunstan*, 2003
6. Lovell-Smith, E. M. Smith, *Old Coaching Days in Otago*, 1931.

The gold escort at Roxburgh. Police escort from left: Constable Bonar, Constable (later Inspector) Fouhy, Sergeant Beaumont. Gold boxes on handcart. *Hocken Library*

CHAPTER 5
Through the Dunstan Gorge

*The buildings in Dunstan
were all composed of sods and calico.*
George Hassing, 1862

The steep-sided Dunstan (now Cromwell) Gorge, where Hartley and Reilly made their famous find, extends 30 kilometres from Clyde to Cromwell. A pioneer prospector, George Hassing,[1] gives us a first-hand description of these early towns in 1862:

> "The buildings in Mutton Town and Dunstan [Clyde] were all composed of sods and calico. [When] the soil of [these] sods became dry, the strong northerly winds [sent] clouds of flying sand sweeping down the long and only street of the Dunstan township, from morning till evening, when the gale generally ceased. The result was that beds, lockers, cupboards and food of every description became smothered with fine sand."

The Mutton Town referred to by Hassing was the 'original' Clyde, a few kilometres south of the definitive town, where sheep from William Fraser's station were slaughtered for the hungry miners. It was soon abandoned for the new town, where the tents of the long street were replaced by hotels and stores.

The original town of Cromwell was "also constructed of sod and calico", Hassing informs us.[1] "But owing to its situation at the foot of a terrace it was not subject to the [wind and] sand nuisance". Sited at the junction of the Clutha and Kawarau Rivers, Cromwell was originally known as "The Junction".

The first road through the Dunstan Gorge was constructed on the west side of the river. But it was subjected to severe washouts and the main road to Queenstown as soon re-routed to the other side.

With the opening of the main road, hostelries and grog dens soon sprang up along the way. Halfway House, halfway

Left: The last people to use the old road on the west side of the Dunstan Gorge before it was flooded by Lake Dunstan. The Otago Goldfields Heritage Trust's cavalcade in November 1991. *Pamela Hall-Jones*

Horse-drawn wagons on the main road to Queenstown on the east side of the Dunstan Gorge, c. 1900.
Alexandra Museum

Halfway House in the Dunstan Gorge, c.1900. Wagons carrying sluice pipes for dredges.
Alexandra Museum

The only known photograph of the original Swan Brewery at Brewery Creek before it was burnt down in 1885. Note state of the main road to Cromwell and Queenstown. *Otago Settlers Museum*

through the gorge, was a popular stopover for travellers and wagoners. Even miners on the west bank of the river crossed by bosun's chair to have a 'tiddle'. The 'dairy' at Dairy Creek was a sly grog shop in disguise, where fiery spirits were sold to the miners. At Champagne Creek, miner William Adams acquired the name of "Champagne Bill", because he shouted champagne to all and sundry, even horses, when he struck gold. At Brewery Creek, just above Hartley and Reilly's famous beach, there was the large two-storeyed Swan Brewery, which supplied the nine hotels of Cromwell and also the outlying district with beer.

Prior to the construction of the Clyde Dam and the flooding of the gorge by Lake Dunstan, archaeologist Neville Ritchie[2] was appointed by the New Zealand Historic Places Trust (from 1977 to 1987) to conduct an archaeological survey of the whole upper Clutha Valley, a huge task. He recorded a total of 44 rock shelters in the Dunstan Gorge, that had been used by gold miners during the nineteenth century. Fortunately most of these rock shelters were on the west side (opposite the main road), so were relatively unfossicked. Three had been used previously by Maori moa-hunters and a number had been lived in by Chinese miners. Most of these shelters and the original roads on each side of the gorge were drowned by the raising of the Clyde Dam.

Also flooded by Lake Dunstan were Cromwell's Chinatown, on the riverbank below Cromwell, and Cornish Point (opposite Cromwell), one of the richest claims in the Cromwell area.

Cromwell's Chinatown on the riverbank below Cromwell, 1908, before it was flooded by Lake Dunstan. Cornish Point on the opposite side of the Kawarau River. *Otago Witness, 1908*

Cromwell's Chinatown

By the time Neville Ritchie[3] 'rediscovered' Cromwell's Chinatown in 1978 it had become completely overgrown by bush and scrub. "Crashing around in the bush with a slasher", Ritchie was pleased to find the site reasonably intact. Two years later he returned to the site with a team of fellow-archaeologists and uncovered an area 200 x 50 metres which was found to contain 30 hut sites, all jumbled closely together. Also stone walls, steps and pathways. There was also what appeared to be an opium den, judging from the amount of opium equipment found there. "It was like uncovering a lost city", Ritchie recalls. The site proved to be a real treasure trove of old Chinese jars, bottles, coins and Chinese ceramics. Cromwell's Chinatown remained a major tourist attraction until it was drowned by Lake Dunstan.

"The Junction"

An historic sketch by John Buchanan during Garvie's survey in 1857 shows a completely bare terrace at "The Junction" (the future Cromwell), the Clutha River continuing into the distance and the Kawarau River coming in from the left.

In 1862 George Hassing[1] and William Docherty arrived at "The Junction". Keen to prospect the Kawarau, Docherty "stripped off, tied his clothes in a neat bundle and lashed these and his tin dish on the top of his head. [Then] he plunged like 'Horatius of old' into the seething waters of the Clutha, below where the Cromwell bridge now stands. He succeeded [in reaching the far side] and getting splendid prospects wherever he tried". A rush to "The Junction" soon ensued.

As George Hassing informs us,[1] the original

Goldfields of Otago

Through the Dunstan Gorge 73

The office of the *Cromwell Argus* newspaper, which is preserved in "Old Cromwell Town" on the waterfront of Lake Dunstan.

Facing page, above: John Buchanan's sketch in 1857 shows a completely bare terrace on the future site of Cromwell at the junction of the Kawarau River (coming in from the left) and the Clutha River, continuing into the distance to Lake Wanaka. *Buchanan's sketchbook.*

Facing page, below: The second footbridge across the Clutha to Cromwell. The foundations of J T. Thomson's traffic bridge in foreground, 1865. *Hocken Library*

town of Cromwell ("The Junction") was constructed of "sod and calico". There being no forest in the area, timber for building had to come all the way from the head of Lake Wanaka and then rafted down the Clutha River. Hassing became one of the pioneer raftsmen on the Clutha, with timber lashed together with flax ropes and a stout manuka pole to steer the raft through the eddies and whirlpools of the wild river. At Cromwell the timber was cut into suitable lengths in sawpits, "enabling the townspeople to erect substantial hotels, stores and residences".

Before Cromwell bridge was built there was a "flat-bottomed punt under the guidance of Old Peter".[1] Then a footbridge built by Henry Hill in 1863. But this was at a low level and was soon washed away. The footbridge was replaced, but suffered the same fate. As Chief Engineer to the province J. T. Thomson was determined to see a permanent traffic bridge at Cromwell. Interestingly his manual on bridge construction[4] shows his original sketch for the solid stone foundations of the bridge that eventuated. Thomson's design for the bridge withstood the ultimate test of the great flood of 1878.

REFERENCES
1. Hassing, George, *The Memory Log of George Hassing*, 1929.
2. Ritchie, Neville, *The Clutha Archaeological Project*, 1977-87.
3. Ritchie, Neville, Interview in *Otago Daily Times*, 31/7/1982.
4. Hall-Jones, John, *John Turnbull Thomson* 1992.

CHAPTER 6
Bannockburn and the Nevis

The Carrick reefs are a modern day Golconda.
Capt. Jackson Barry, 1869

Prior to the construction of the road through the Dunstan (Cromwell) Gorge the easiest route to the Upper Clutha Valley was along the open tops of the Cairnmuir Range, high above the west side of the gorge. The pioneers of this route, which later became a packhorse track (and now a DOC walking track), were two prospectors, Edward Cornish[1] and Fred Pope.

After the Great Flood of September 1862 Cornish and Pope traversed the Cairnmuir Range in October, descending at the far end at Cornish Point (giving us the probable origin[1] of this name). Continuing up the west bank of the Kawarau River they crossed the flat at the mouth of the Bannockburn to discover the rich alluvial goldfield on the Pipeclay Terraces beyond. Other prospectors soon followed and when gold was discovered in the Bannockburn itself, the original township of Bannockburn was formed on the flat at the mouth of the Bannockburn. Later this shifted up to its present site on the terrace above the flat, where the old Bannockburn Hotel and other historic buildings have recently been restored. This

Old sluicings at Cairnmuir, near Cornish Point.

Bannockburn Hotel, c.1900, Donald McRae, proprietor. *Alexandra Museum*

second location for Bannockburn tended to spread further up the Bannockburn Valley when the Bannockburn to Nevis Road was constructed.

The Carrick Range mines

Forming a mountain backdrop to Bannockburn, the Carrick Range rises in rounded contours from the Pipeclay Terraces and Kawarau River, inserting itself between the Bannockburn Valley and the Nevis Valley to its west. Soon after the discovery of the alluvial gold in the Pipeclay Terraces a number of gold-bearing quartz reefs were discovered higher up on the Carrick Range. Most of these reefs were very broken with faults and lay dormant until 'rediscovered' in 1869 by the flamboyant Captain Jackson Barry of Cromwell who pronounced them as a "modern day Golconda" (an ancient city of India renowned for its diamond mines).

By 1872 there were three quartz crushing batteries[1] operating on the Carrick Range and by 1876 there were five with a total of 35 stamps. With all this activity on the Carrick Range a number of satellite gold towns sprang up on the range, all completely dependent for supplies on the 'mother' town of Bannockburn down in the valley below. These tiny townships were linked to Bannockburn by a "frightful" dray road (still a deeply rutted road) which ascended the main ridge line.

Stewart Town

For six long years the great sluicing potential of the Pipeclay Terraces lay dormant. Lack of water for sluicing was the great obstacle to recovering this rich alluvial

Sluiced cliff-face at Pipeclay Terraces. Sludge channel in centre.

Massive chimney and stone walls of Menzies and Stewart's cottage at Stewart Town, 2005

gold. Then in 1868 two Scotsmen, David Menzies and John Stewart, dug a water race from Long Gully to a storage dam, Menzies Dam on Menzies Terrace, at the head of Pipeclay Gully and the massive sluicing of the Pipeclay Terraces got under way. Later the Carrick water race was brought in from high on the Carrick Range, adding greatly to the massive sluicing operations in Pipeclay Gully, so much so that a tail race had to be dug to get rid of the growing accumulation of tailings. Both Stewart and Menzies were bachelors and lived together in their stone cottage (which is still standing) beside Menzies Dam on Menzies Terrace. Other miners built their cottages nearby and the little settlement became known as Stewart Town.

Today, the huge sculptured Bannockburn sluicings are one of the most spectacular areas of sluicings in New Zealand. Now a DOC reserve, a detailed trail guide is available for a self-guided walk.

Quartzville

As might be expected the enthusiastic Captain Jackson Barry was the first to form a company, the Royal Standard Co, to place the first quartz crushing battery on the Carrick Range. Strategically sited at the foot of the leading ridge of the Carrick Range and the "frightful" dray road up the ridge, the Royal Standard battery was in an excellent position to service not only its own mine, but could be hired by all other mines working the Carrick reefs higher up. And so in 1870 the township of Quartzville evolved around the Royal Standard battery. Opposite the battery John McCormack built his Carrick Range Hotel. Other hotels and shops soon appeared and in 1871 William Sutherland established his blacksmith's shop.

Unhappily, because of the broken nature of the Carrick Range reefs, none of the mines did well and by 1877 Quartzville began to close down. The Carrick Range Hotel was shifted down to Bannockburn and other businesses drifted away. Today there is little to be seen at the site of Quartzville, only the remains of William Sutherland's blacksmith shop, which has been identified by archaeologist Neville Ritchie.

Carricktown

One year after Quartzville was founded another gold town, Carricktown, was established halfway up the Carrick Ridge, to serve a number of mines which were being worked in that area. Prominent among these

The Carrick water race, which is still used today for irrigation.

The huge water wheel of the Young Australian mine.

mines were the Elizabeth, the first (1869) mine at Carricktown, which had a battery of eight stamps, the Star, which had a battery of ten stamps and the Heart of Oak mine. The Star battery was initially driven by a coal-burning boiler until the Carrick water race was dug and worked co-operatively with the Heart of Oak mine to crush its ore. The combined Star and Heart of Oak mines were still working in 1899 and were the most productive mines at Carricktown[1]. The remains of their mullock heaps can still be seen, just up the road from Carricktown.

By 1871 Carricktown had become a busy little gold town of three hotels, two stores, a butchery, and a bakery, as well as a number of miners' huts. With no firewood available on the bare mountainside 25 tons of coal had to be carted up to the rutted mountain road each week to supply the quartz crushing batteries and the town. An expensive business. For the coal-fired batteries it must have been a huge relief when water power became available from the Carrick water race. Today the stone shells of half-a-dozen huts can be seen at the site of Carricktown.

Young Australian

The Young Australian reef was further up the ridge from Carricktown, at the head of Adams Gully. The reef was discovered by a prospector named Jackson (?an Australian). A company was formed and in 1871 a shaft was sunk to mine the reef. But for the first three years all the ore had to be carted down to the batteries below for crushing. With the prospect of the Carrick water race coming on stream in 1875 a battery with a huge 7.9 metre iron water wheel was transported from Conroys Gully by a local character by the name of Jeremiah Drummy. The battery and water wheel were erected conveniently close to the Young Australian mine and in 1875 water from the Carrick race began turning the giant wheel to crush the ore on location, instead of having to cart it all the way downhill.

For the first year of operations fortune smiled on the Young Australian battery, yielding over an ounce of gold per ton of quartz crushed, then the reef ran out. For the next ten years the battery worked intermittently with variable success under different owners, including the well known Frenchman, Louis Jean Hubert. The five stamper battery was transferred across to the opposite side of Adams Gully where it was operated by a Pelton wheel.

During the 1990s, nearly all the wood of the Young Australian water wheel was renewed, so that the giant wheel still stands in solitary splendour at the head of Adams Gully. A scramble across to the opposite side of the gully leads to the transferred five

Berdan of the Young Australian mine, 1979.

Restored miner's hut at the Young Australian mine, 1979.

The five stamper battery of the Young Australian mine, 1979.

Nevis Crossing Hotel. *Courtesy Ron Murray*

Right: Remaining wall of Nevis Crossing Hotel, next to Ben Nevis cattleyards, 2005.

stamper battery and a restored miner's hut.

With all this mining activity in an around Bannockburn, the town for a transient period outshone Cromwell as the centre of gold mining in the district. Until the road was constructed through the Cromwell Gorge all supplies from down country were packed by horse over the Cairnmuir track from Clyde to Bannockburn. The town was also an important access and supply centre for the Nevis Valley goldfields. Bannockburn was connected to Cromwell by a ferry across the Kawarau River and in 1874 the ferry was replaced by the Bannockburn bridge, which only four years later was washed away in the Great Flood of 1878.

Once the road through the Dunstan Gorge was completed all this quickly changed and Cromwell became a flourishing main town at the junction of the roads to Queenstown and Wanaka.

THE NEVIS

The long flat valley of the Nevis River rises steadily from its mouth at the Kawarau River to it source on Garston Hill (1,100 metres). Flanked by high mountain ranges on each side the Nevis Valley (or simply The Nevis, as it is commonly known) is divided into a distinctive Lower Nevis plain and an Upper Nevis plain by a constriction in the middle, the rugged Nevis Gorge. Because of continual slips and washouts only the Lower Nevis can be reached safely by car. Departing from Bannockburn the road ascends steeply to Duffers Saddle (1,300 metres) in the Carrick Range, where wagons returning to Bannockburn used to drag large rock slabs at the end of steel chains to act as brakes. It is said that the Carrick station woolshed at the foot of the hill was constructed from these discarded rock slabs.

Beyond Duffers Saddle the road descends

Chinese miners' schist and sacking hut in Potters Gully. Rev. George McNeur on right. Note typical Chinese rounded chimney next to doorway.
Alexander Turnbull library

steeply to cross the Nevis River at Nevis Crossing, where there was once a town of that name. The road continues across the Lower Nevis plain to the other township in the valley, Lower Nevis. But from the Nevis Gorge onwards it is very much a 4WD road, with the hazards of slips, washouts and closures by now.

With the remains of sluicings, dredge ponds and miners' stone huts all along the way, a journey through the Nevis Valley is like a step back in time to the old gold mining days. During two summer vacations in the early 1980s by wife, Pamela and I trekked the full length of the Nevis Valley, which she, as a Scot, identifies with Glen Nevis in the shadow of Ben Nevis in Scotland. Pamela rode her horse, Suellen, while I chose the safer surety of 'Shanks' pony', both enjoying the peace and tranquillity of this magnificent valley, away from the 'madding crowd'.

As we descended from Duffers Saddle we looked down on the Nevis Valley far below, the buildings of Ben Nevis station in the immediate foreground, the Lower Nevis township in the middle distance and the Nevis Gorge beyond. Arriving at Nevis Crossing we spotted the remains of a wall of the "Nevis Crossing Hotel", next to the old Ben Nevis cattleyards. In its heyday Nevis Crossing was a thriving township with three hotels, stores and shops and a large population of Chinese miners,[1] who lived apart in their own "Chinese camp" with their own stores.[2]

From Nevis Crossing I detoured down the Nevis River to the gully of Potters No. 1 Creek, where in 1862 the indomitable John Lishman Potter discovered the first gold in the Nevis Valley, on his way to the Nokomai goldfield in Southland. Later there was a little settlement of 20 Chinese miners in Potters Gully.

Continuing on to Lower Nevis township we came first to Schoolhouse Creek where Gavine McLean (see later) used to teach at the Nevis school (founded in 1874). Near the junction of Schoolhouse Creek lie a few timbers of the small *Nevis Crossing* dredge, the dredge with the longest working life in the whole of Otago and Southland and probably New Zealand.[3] For the dredges working in The Nevis is was a godsend when coal was discovered at Nevis Crossing, eliminating the expensive cartage of coal over Duffers Saddle.

Arriving at the Lower Nevis township we viewed the ruins of the "Nevis Hotel" and also noted that one or two of the cottages were still lived in. At the cemetery, the second for the area, were a few marked graves, the earliest dating from the 1890s. In its heyday the population for the whole Nevis Valley peaked at 600 in 1866,[1] of which nearly half were Chinese miners, who later outnumbered the Europeans. A handwritten newspaper, the *Nevis Buster*, was produced weekly at Lower Nevis and posted up for all to read. There

The original wooden Nevis Hotel. After it was burnt down the owners moved into their stone house opposite, which then became the new Nevis Hotel.
Courtesy Ron Murray

Right: Ruins of the second Nevis Hotel, 1981.
Pamela Hall-Jones

was also a regular mail run by horse and gig from Bannockburn to The Nevis, but sometimes the valley would be cut off for weeks with deep snow on Duffers Saddle.

Approaching the Nevis Gorge we forded Commissioners Creek, the source of five water races for sluicing and hydraulic elevating. The lower races provided water at low pressure for ground sluicing, while the higher races delivered water under the high pressure necessary for elevating.

At the entrance of the gorge we saw the stacked stones of this once large Chinese claim. Throughout the length of the gorge we spotted the remains of diversion channels, heaped stones and stone huts, evidence of the Chinese and European miners who once worked in the gorge.

Exiting from the Nevis Gorge we crossed Whittens Creek, where the stone walls of W. O'Connell's "Loch Linnhe" station homestead and stables of the 1880s stand on the far bank. After O'Connell abandoned the homestead, miners and dredgemen moved into the warmth and shelter of this solid stone building.

We were now confronted with the huge sluiced mound of Baileys Hill (named after an early miner, John Bailey). On the far side were delighted to meet up with Ian and Gavine McLean, whose family had been

Diversion channel in Nevis Gorge.

Remains of Loch Linnhe homestead at Whittens Creek, 1981

sluicing the hill since the 1930s, "We winter in Milton and summer in The Nevis", they told us. They were comfortably set up in their cosy little hut with their own 'home-made' electricity from a generator run by a tractor and their own power line. "I was fresh from Christchurch Training College when I was appointed teacher at Lower Nevis school in 1927", she told us. She kept in touch with "all her boys" when they went away to the War and was deeply saddened when some of them were killed. When I mentioned how badly the gold miners' tailings had scarred the landscape she gently rebuked me. "Tailings are lovely", she said. A phrase I will never forget, and so true when you see the beautiful patterns of herring-bone tailings. I begged her to record her memories of the mining days and was delighted when she did so:[4]

"The homes of the miners were very similar to those of coal miners in earlier years. Small and quite well-built with four rooms, no bathroom, an outside toilet and often additional bedrooms with inferior studs and finish, being added as the family grew in number. Most of the Nevis houses had been erected towards the end of the nineteenth century and showed the effects of the summer heat and winter blizzards. Except for the hotel the clothes washing was done outside by the womenfolk, an outdoor copper being used on cold days to heat the water. The hotel had a wash-house with a copper and tubs and Monday was always their washing day.

"The family had their morning wash outside in a watertub and in winter the ice had to be hammered until it broke. Hands were dipped gingerly into the icy cold water and a little splash was directed to the eyes and mouth, this lick and a promise brought the wash to a swift finish.

"Furniture was very simple, though some of the

Bannockburn and the Nevis

The McLeans' settlement at the foot of Baileys Hill, 1981.

chairs and duchesses would be prized today. Iron beds were often old with missing knobs and the seating problem would be solved with a long wooden form behind the table. There would be a stove, years and years old which stood on legs in an alcove and provided warmth in winter for all the family as they were able to sit around the front, back and sides. 'Cow chips' supplemented the coal, and miners working on the peat bogs dried the peat and used it for fuel.

"The managing ability of most women on the goldfield can be marvelled at. Money was often scarce especially in winter time when some of the men were unemployed. Nothing was ever wasted and milk was used as the basis of many meals. The children who had no organised games spent their spare time working for the family as soon as they were old enough. When the wild gooseberries were ripe they gathered dozens and dozens of kilos for jam-making. They went rabbiting with dogs and traps; the skins were sold and the carcases were food for themselves and the pigs. They gathered wood which was scarce and cow and horse manure which was not. The milking cows often wandered many miles and it was the job of the children to find them and bring them home.

"These children didn't complain, because they were not aware that their way of life was any different from that of their fellows outside the valley."

From the McLean's cottage a little concrete shed can be seen further up the valley. I remembered it well because I had used it as

Series of dredge ponds in the Upper Nevis Valley. Baileys Hill beyond.

Goldfields of Otago

Concrete foundations of the powerhouse for the Earnscleugh No. 3 dredge, 2005.

an overnight shelter when I first tramped into the valley from Garston in 1981 and spent one of the coldest nights I have ever had in my life. They chuckled when I told them about my experience the next morning. "It used to be a generator shed for the dredges", they informed me, "but it was so cold inside that afterwards we used it as a freezer". No wonder I had nearly frozen to death that night!

Continuing up the Upper Nevis Valley we passed a series of dredge ponds and the foundations of the power house for the old *Earnscleugh No. 3* dredge,[3] which worked there after being dismantled and shifted from Alexandra in 1926. There were also other dredges working in the area as evidenced by the number of ponds and tailings.

Further on we came to the large sluiced basin created by hydraulic elevating. This was John Williamson's party who worked there during the 1930s to 1948. The remains of their stone huts still stand at the edge of the basin.

Near the head of the Upper Nevis Valley we arrived at the Roaring Lion hut at the junction of the Roaring Lion Creek with the Nevis River. We now began the ascent of Garston Hill, criss-crossing the source of the Nevis River on the way. Arriving at the saddle with the head of Nokomai Valley we spotted some iron fluming from the Roaring Lion water race, which Chinese miners had constructed all the way, in and out of gullies, from Roaring Lion Creek. The Roaring Lion water race, which was maintained by Chinese race men living in their sod huts, was the key to high pressure elevating in the gold rich Nokomai Valley in Southland. We descended the Garston Hill to Garston, the end of our trek through The Nevis in the footsteps of the gold miners of yesteryear.

REFERENCES
1. Parcell, J. C., *Heart of the Desert*, 1951.
2. Ng, Dr James, *Windows on a Chinese Past*, 1995.
3. Hamel, Jill, *The Archaeology of Otago*, 2001
4. McLean, Gavine, *the Mining Memories of Gavine McLean*.

Ngapara No. 2 dredge working in the Upper Nevis Valley.
Courtesy Ron Murray

Miners' stone huts at the edge of the hydraulic elevating hole of John Williamson's claim.

Right: Chinese race man seated outside his sod hut in Nokomai Valley. *Hocken Library*

Ruins of Chinese sod hut in Nokomai Valley. *Southland Museum*

CHAPTER 7
The Rich Reefs of Bendigo

The saloons became crowded with diggers in the evenings, when the shouting, drinking and yelling was something to astonish the new chum.
George Hassing, Wakefield, 1862

Oddly enough it wasn't the prospectors pushing their way up the Clutha River Valley from Cromwell who discovered the gold in the Bendigo Creek tributary of the river. It was a party of miners who came through Thomsons Gorge in the Dunstan Mountains in late 1862 who discovered the alluvial gold in Bendigo Creek.

Soon there were "about 150 miners"[1] working in the gorge of Bendigo Creek and George Hassing, with an eye for business, took over the ferry across the Clutha River at Rocky Point, near the mouth of Bendigo Creek. A tiny township, Wakefield, formed at the ferry landing, where the Wakefield Ferry Hotel was started by Sam Box,[1] "a tough old Cornishman and his estimable wife, an Irish lady with a captivating and persuasive brogue.

Sam Box and his son, Sam, also did the packing from the ferry. Other saloons speedily followed under the ownership of Charles Hare, Joe Smith and Mrs J. Wilson, wife of 'Jack the Drummer'. These saloons became crowded in the evenings, when the shouting, drinking and yelling was something to astonish the new chum." A butchery was started by 'Sydney Bill' (William Smith) and a second-hand shop by 'Johnny All Sorts'.

Most of the alluvial mining on the Bendigo goldfield took place in Bendigo Creek itself, its Aurora Creek branch and a tributary of the latter, Swipers Creek, a strange name which was acquired in the following way, as George Hassing relates:[1]

"In the upper part of the gully, which was the richest and shallowest ground, were located some

Rocky Point Hotel, Wakefield. Built in 1867 the hotel was destroyed by fire in 1905. *G. Duff*

Bendigo township, 1936. The furthermost stone building is the old bakery.
Courtesy Ron Murray

Below: The ruins of the stone bakery photographed from the same angle in 2004

twenty-five miners, hard-working, honest fellows, but wonderful 'boozers'. This upper reach was known as 'Swipers Row'. Each Saturday forenoon the boxes were washed up. Dinner and a wash-up followed. Then all hands would troop down to Box's store to sell the week's gold, buy next week's tucker, have two or three drinks each and return to the camp, each carrying a couple of bottles of liquid stimulant. On arrival at the camp a big bonfire of manuka would be lit, the liquid pooled and the fun started. It generally commenced with vocal music, but as the liquid diminished and the hours grew later, the singing increased in volume till it became a hideous, demoniacal yelling that entirely overpowered and drowned every sound within a radius of a mile or so. Frequently on a Saturday evening, though three miles away, I heard the echo of the jollifications at Swipers' Row wafted on the evening air like the sound of reverberating billows breaking against a rock-bound shore.

"These were hard-working, honest miners. At any rate I found them so. But the indulgence in, and the love of liquor, made the best of men depraved. This was evidenced on one occasion when on a Friday night the sluice-boxes in Swipers' Row were swept clean by a flood and the usual Saturday's gold could not be obtained. A consultation was held, when it was decided to proceed to the store as usual and raise an alarm of fire. While the crowd was at the store, one of the miners set fire to an empty straw-thatched hut some distance down the gully. An alarm was raised by the crowd, and all including Mr and Mrs Box went to the rescue. Then 'Harry the Slogger' nipped into the saloon, dexterously emptied the contents of the cashbox into his pocket and disappeared. On their return to the store it was found that a robbery had been committed, but the culprit remained a mystery, and the boys in the Row had their usual concert and spree in the evening."

From Wakefield a 'road' led across the flat to the mouth of the Bendigo Gully, where William Goodall established his Bendigo Gully Hotel and store[2] on the site of the future township of Bendigo. A second hotel followed, the Solway, also a general store, butchery and bakery. In 1869 the township of Bendigo was officially laid out at the foot of Bendigo Hill, with a main street, York Street, 500 metres long. Today only a few ruins remain at the site of the old town of Bendigo. William Goodall's hotel was burnt down, but the Solway Hotel and garden are marked by a heap of stones among the trees on the south side of 'York Street'. On the opposite side of the 'street' are the more obvious stone walls of the bakery.

Logan's reef

The early phase of alluvial mining at Bendigo was short-lived, from 1862 to 1866. It was the discovery of the gold rich Cromwell reef by Thomas Logan (hence the popular

George Goodger of Cromwell who financed the purchase of the Solway battery. *J. C. Parcell*

name of Logan's reef)[4] that made Bendigo famous. Vincent Pyke[3] later described it as "undoubtedly the richest quartz reef in Otago. Some parts of it yielded as much as six ounces of gold to the ton, and as the stone was generally friable, great quantities of it could be extracted and put through the stamper daily."

In 1863 Thomas Logan[2] located several lines of gold bearing reefs, including the rich Cromwell (Logan's) reef, on Bendigo Hill above Bendigo, but Logan was unable to develop them because of a lack of capital. In 1865 Julian Coates reported the reefs to a group of Dunedin businessmen, who formed a company which took up a large block of the reefs including Logan's Cromwell reef. Logan thought they were treating him unfairly and retaliated by deliberately losing the line of the reef. The Dunedin syndicate soon tired of the lack of profit and dropped the claim, which Logan promptly took up again.

Logan's rich Cromwell reef had got off to a bad start and was dubbed a 'duffer' by all those who did not know the inside story. Logan pottered on at his reef with the two mates, William Garrett and Brian Hebden. The latter was otherwise known as "Charcoal Joe", because he used to temper the picks of the miners at his charcoal burner. None of the trio had money to invest in developing the reef and kept their income flowing by working intermittently on their alluvial claims. Then in 1868 the trio showed their quartz samples to George Goodger, an hotel-keeper at Cromwell. Goodger was a Californian who knew something about quartz gold and he recognised the value of their samples. He joined the partnership and put up the money to buy a quartz crushing battery.

A twelve stamper battery from Hindon was erected at the foot of the Bendigo Gorge so that there would be a good head of water to drive it. The disadvantage was that the ore from the Cromwell reef had to be carted two

Stone ruins and old cart on the flat at Logantown.

Ruins of Pengelly's Hotel at Welshtown.

Miner's hut on the crest of the hill at Welshtown.

kilometres downhill by a rough dray road to the Solway battery (as it was named) at Bendigo for crushing. The initial crushing in May 1869 returned 238 ounces of gold for ten days' work.[2] Such a good result hit the headlines in the newspapers and the second rush to Bendigo began. For the first six months of 1870 the crushings produced a total of 8,129 ounces of gold, paying out enormous dividends to the four partners in the Cromwell Quartz Mining Co., as they called their company.

By 1869 the miners had become tired of plodding daily all the way up the steep hill from Bendigo to the mine, then back again in the evening. So a new township, Logantown, was formed on the flat immediately below the mine. Named after Thomas Logan, the town was an irregular line of corrugated iron buildings, three hotels, stores, a butchery and a bakery, as well as miners' huts scattered along the dray road.

Above the mine, on the crest of Bendigo Hill, was another township, Welshtown, so named because of its predominance of Welsh miners. Welshtown was essentially a cluster of miners' huts, the exception being William Pengelly's Hotel across the gully of Swipers Creek.

There was still no surveyed road from Bendigo up to the mine, so the Cromwell Quartz Mining Co was saddled with the burden of having to maintain their own dray road. What with the excellent profits the company was making from the mine it was decided to shift its Solway battery up to the main shaft of the mine so that the ore could be processed on location. The Aurora battery in Aurora Creek was acquired to add to a new 20 stamper battery, which would be driven by steam power fired by coal. Appropriately the newly constructed "Matilda" battery was named after Matilda Goodger, daughter of the original investor in the mine, George Goodger, and 'christened' by Matilda at an opening ceremony in December 1878.

Matilda battery and No. 1 minehead perched precariously on the steep hillside. *Hocken Library*

Machine house and poppet head of No. 2 shaft. *Hocken Library*

A new shaft, No. 2, was sunk from which the company was to make its main profit. The shaft was huge, 2.7 x 1.2 metres across and was sunk to a depth of 78 metres. A poppet head was constructed over the minehead, which was surrounded by a machine house, smithy, carpenters' shop and offices.

The new Matilda battery rapidly justified its existence, recovering 4,086 ounces of gold for the first six months and 8,118 ounces for the first year. Thereafter the returns tended to drop off and what with problems with flooding and a miners' strike, the original owners sold out in 1884 to a new company. During their ownership of the mine the four partners had obtained half a million pounds worth of gold.[2] Sadly, of the four only Brian Hebden, the humble charcoal burner, lived to enjoy his prosperity. He returned to England where he set up a successful business. George Goodger, the benefactor, committed suicide over financial matters. William Garrett, the mine manager, died at 31 after being thrown from a horse and Thomas Logan, the discoverer, invested unwisely and died a poor man.

Thereafter the mine pottered on intermittently under various owners with variable success, but with production tending to taper off, until it finally closed down in 1938.

In 1908 ten stampers from the battery were shifted across to Thomsons Gorge to construct the Come in Time battery. The returns from the Come in Time battery for its first year of operations were disappointing[2] and it closed down. A second attempt was made in 1909, but with the return of a meagre 4 ounces of gold the battery ceased work. After one final fling in 1919 with similar results it closed down permanently. Nevertheless the Come in Time battery still stands proudly at the foot of a gully just off the road through Thomsons Gorge.

The 'last' miner[4] at Bendigo was a Second War veteran, Wattie Thompson, who lived in his little hut on the bank of Bendigo Creek near the old town. For three long years he laboured single-handed at stacking a huge pile of boulders along the bank of the creek with the aim of getting down to the pay dirt at the bottom, only to have it buried beneath a deep layer of stones in a flash flood. A

Come in Time battery, Thomsons Gorge, 2004.

Wattie Thompson standing beside his boulder wall in Bendigo Creek. His cradle and sluice box in foreground, his hut behind. *June Wood*

loner and deeply religious man he lived close to nature. In 1979 he purchased a ticket with his hard-won earnings for a flight over the Antarctic, only to perish in the disastrous Mt Erebus crash.

When viewed today from the flat at Bendigo township the road up the hill to Logantown and Welshtown appears dauntingly steep. However it is no real problem for ordinary cars and well worth the effort. Where the steep section flattens out look left for two old drays and some crumbling ruins, which are

Foundations of machine house at No.2 shaft, 2004.

Stone archway across Aurora Creek.

all that remain of the important service town of Logantown. Continue uphill to the less important, but more spectacular, ruins of the miners' huts at Welshtown, on the summit of Bendigo Hill. From here, fine views of the surrounding mountains are obtained.

The walker is now faced with two options, a long loop track across Swipers Gully to Pengelly's Hotel and on round Aurora Creek to Logantown, with a magnificent stone archway across Aurora Creek on the way, or a shorter descent through the workings of the Cromwell Quartz Mining Co. to the site of the Matilda battery.

The motorist returning downhill should stop at the carpark at the No. 2 mine shaft.

Today only the foundations of the machine house and smithy and a huge pile of tailings remain. The opening of the 178 metre shaft has been covered over with a heavy iron frame. Continue down the old dray track that was used to cart the ore down to the Matilda battery, about 200 metres downhill, where the foundations of the battery and some stone ruins will be seen.

Quartz Reef Point

J. C. Parcell[2] records that in 1865 there were 60 miners working at Quartz Reef Point, just four kilometres north of Cromwell on the road to Bendigo. Little is known of what luck they and their successors had, but the tidy stacking of the stone walls for their sluicing channels has left a beautiful pattern of herring-bone tailings along the terrace above Quartz Reef Point on Northburn station. An example of what Gavine McLean of the Nevis meant when she said "tailings are lovely".

On the top of the terrace there used to be holding dams for the water for sluicing, but these have now been bulldozed away. There is also an old Chinese stone hut near the tailings, but this has recently become heavily overgrown with briar making it difficult to find.

REFERENCES
1. Hassing, George, *The Memory Log of George Hassing*, 1929
2. Parcell, J. C. *Heart of the Desert*, 1951
3. Pyke, Vincent, *Early Gold Discoveries in Otago*, 1887
4. Duff, Geoffrey, *Sheep may safely graze*, 1978

The Rich Reefs of Bendigo 93

Herring-bone tailings at Quartz Reef Point.

Right: Chinese stone hut at Quartz Reef Point, 1986.

CHAPTER 8
The Dry Cardrona

*Motorists driving over the Crown Range
were rationed to one beer,
those heading for Wanaka were allowed two.*
"One up, two down"

In October 1862 it was rumoured that "a miner named Fox had discovered a goldfield of surpassing richness in some remote and unexplored region".[1] Numbers of miners set out in quest of the new field, but for a time their search was baffled, until Michael Grogan and his party stumbled across four pennyweights of gold that had been dropped on the cattle track up the Cardrona Valley:

> "On 9 November, whilst a crowd of diggers were camped on the banks of the Cardrona, Mullins and myself took a walk to see how that part of the country looked, and in walking along the river where what I called a slide had occurred, there had been a track formed by the cattle. I, being a little further up the creek, sat down until Mullins came up. He immediately told me that some person must have lost some gold, and produced about 4 pennyweight, that he got on the cattle track. We still continued up the creek, until we thought it time to return to our camping-ground; and on our way back he showed me the place, but on searching for more we could get none, and from the appearance of the black soil we certainly thought that it must have been lost by Fox or some other person."[1]

Two days later Grogan and his mates returned to the spot where Mullins had picked up the four pennyweights of "dropped" gold, and on "breaking up the surface" of the riverbank Grogan discovered three pennyweights of gold. That afternoon the party "nuggeted out" over nine ounces of gold.

Although Grogan's party had not found Fox's rich goldfield (at Arrowtown, see next chapter) they nevertheless had the consolation of discovering their own goldfield in the Cardrona Valley. An interesting witness to Grogan's discovery was Dr James Hector (later Sir James), the provincial geologist, who continued up the Cardrona Valley and

George Hassing, prospector, ferryman, storekeeper and teacher, who lived to the age of 91.
G. Hassing

over the Crown Range (1,076 metres) to Arrowtown to find Fox's party and "about forty others, quietly working away in a secluded gorge of the Arrow River".[1]

Many miners hastened to the new Cardrona goldfield, but the fame of the Cardrona was soon eclipsed by the discoveries of the gold-rich Arrow and Shotover Rivers (see later chapters). Whereas the mining population of the Cardrona Valley grew to about a thousand, many prospectors passed through

The Dry Cardrona

in silent contempt using Cardrona merely as a convenient 'stopover' on the way to the golden rivers of the Lake Wakatipu Basin.

George Hassing's account

Thanks again to George Hassing[2] we have a lucid account of the Cardrona goldfield and the early township of Cardrona.

Prior to moving to Cardrona in 1863, George Hassing had a whaleboat ferry for crossing the Clutha River at Albert Town. Then with the rush to the Cardrona Valley and "Fox's" at Arrowtown, Hassing prudently shifted his ferry business downriver to Sandy Point, which cut 20 kilometres off the miners' trek to the Cardrona Valley and "Fox's". At Sandy Point, Hassing also established a store, where the local miners used to congregate on Saturday evenings for a drink and a yarn. What with the variety of talent among the assembled crowd they were interesting evenings indeed:

> "There was Thomas Hope Baird [grandson of Sir David Baird who slew the infamous Tippoo Sahib in India]; he was a book of knowledge on India, Egypt, Palestine, and on any subject with an Oriental flavour. To him the miners used to listen with rapt attention: 'the dropping of a pound note on the clay floor would strike the ear with a dull thud'. The silence was broken only by the necessary whisper, just sufficiently loud – 'Fill 'em up again, please'. An outstanding character was the self-styled James Alexander Gordon-Cumming McIntosh Urquhart, known for short as the marquis, who hailed from Kinbachie in Sutherlandshire. He was a fluent, authority on yachting in the Mediterranean and off the coast of Norway. Also among the group were Orr and Mackay, qualified medical practitioners, overflowing always with Latin quotations. There was Captain Pearce, a retired British Army officer, and Kenneth Stewart, a squatter from Australia, and Charles Cameron, a Highlander as impetuous as he was intrepid, who discovered the Haast Pass [before Julius von Haast 'officially' did so]."

Once the Cromwell bridge was completed the traffic to Cardrona and "Fox's" went by way of the Roaring Meg track in the Kawarau Gorge. Hassing's business at Sandy Point dropped off quickly and accordingly he moved to Cardrona.

"In 1863 a township was laid out", Hassing informs us. (Logically the town took its name from the Cardrona River, which surveyor J. T. Thomson had named in 1857 after Cardrona House[3] and the Cardrona Forest on the Scottish Border). "Several canvas-

Miners at a dangerous crossing on the Roaring Meg track to Cardrona. Painting by J. T Thomson.
Hall-Jones family

Cardrona House, Scotland, the origin of J. T. Thomson's name for the Cardrona River.

covered sod buildings were erected for stores and saloons. These shortly gave place to structures made of timber with iron roofs, and a very busy lively little township sprang up."

"Most of the gold was obtained from above the township, but in 1865 rich gold was opened a mile or so below the town. The three principal claims were the Gin and Raspberry [doubtless named after the favourite drink of the day], Pirate and Homeward Bound. These are all alluvial claims worked by shafts and drives or tunnels, 24-30 feet below the surface. [The returns were good] so the little town was just booming. Four hotels and as many billiard saloons were doing a roaring trade and everyone had a pocket full of money. Balls, races and carnivals were held and everyone went the 'full hog'."

"The West Coast rush, however, caused many who were doing really well to clear out and in 1867, when all the rich claims had been worked out, the miners left in almost a body. Then the Chinese influx took place, with some 600 Chinamen taking up the whole creek bed in open-faced, large and deep paddocks. These Celestials, working like bees in a hive, did uncommonly well and three

Robert McDougall's store and post office at Cardrona, 2004.

large Chinese stores, cookshops and gambling dens were erected in the township. It reminded one both in odour and appearance of the outskirts of Canton."

"In the late 1860s European miners struck a lead of gold in a flat a mile below the township, at a depth of 30 feet. Here two large claims were opened out, the Empire [where Hassing was the principal owner] and

La Franchi's dredge working in Tuohys Gully, Cardrona. *Lakes District Museum*

the Banner of War, and were worked by inclines and tunnels. What became known as the lower township sprang up here, with its [own] hotel, store and many neat miners' residences."

"In the early 1870s the whole of Branch Creek, a tributary of the Cardrona four miles below the township, was pegged off for hydraulic sluicing. [This] creek yielded a lot of gold for several years. Then in 1878 the Great Flood overwhelmed the place, gutting and filling up the workings with thousands of tons of tailings, especially on the lower flat. Thus catastrophe ruined many of the miners, myself included, and I [turned to teaching at Cardrona and later Southland for the next 42 years]." On Christmas Day 1928, George Magnus Hassing, the Danish sailor, prospector, ferryman, storekeeper and teacher died at Riverton Hospital, aged 91.

One of Hassing's closest friends was Robert McDougall, storekeeper, postmaster and registrar at Cardrona. "An educated, energetic and enterprising man, he worked on the Australian goldfields and thoroughly identified himself with the fortunes of the miners. No hard up digger went short of tucker if McDougall heard about it."[2] His son Robert McDougall jnr. took over the store and post office, which had been built in 1871 and is still standing at Cardrona.

Another friend was Alfred ("Alf") La Franchi from Switzerland who ran an hotel at Lower Cardrona, but in 1897 ventured into dredging instead. Unlike the other Cardrona dredges which worked in the main riverbed, La Franchi's dredge floated on a pond at the foot of Tuohys Gully, on John Lee's present snow farm. The pond was kept full by a pipeline off the Mt Pisa Range and the dredge was driven by an ingenious system of a nozzle from the pipeline playing on a Pelton wheel. For a time La Franchi's dredge returned seven ounces of gold a week, but in 1916 its rafting pontoons finally gave up the ghost and the dredge sank in ignominy in the mud of its own pond.

Cardrona Hotel

The photogenic facade of the Cardrona Hotel makes it one of the best recognised hotels in the whole of New Zealand. Built in 1870 the hotel has had a number of owners over the years, but the last before it lost its

90 year old James Paterson who kept a stern discipline at the Cardrona Hotel bar.
Alexander Turnbull Library

licence in 1861, James Paterson, would be the best known name of all. An ex-miner, James Paterson took over the hotel in 1926 and in latter years he was remembered as a bald-headed, bespectacled barman in braces who served warm beer from a corked bottle, up to the age of 90. Paterson kept a firm discipline in his bar. He was never keen on serving women and he rationed patrons about to drive over the Crown Range to one glass of beer, but those heading down to Wanaka were allowed two. From this the popular song evolved, "One up, two down". The Licensing Commission were suitably impressed with the stern discipline that James Paterson kept in

Cardrona Hotel in the 1920s. *Lakes District Museum*

The Cardrona Hotel today.

Old sluicings in the Cardrona Valley. Mt Pisa Range on skyline.

his bar and waived the cessation of the hotel's licence while he remained owner. He died aged 91 and was buried alongside his wife Ettie (née La Franchi) at the little cemetery at Lower Cardrona. Here too lies the Irish fiddler, Paddy Galvin, who used to play at the bar and the tombstone of the Swiss family, La Franchi.

Protected by the Historic Places Trust the hotel has recently undergone some major renovations, including the construction of a large dining room behind the hotel's facade.

With the recent restoration of the licence to the Cardrona Hotel, why is it still the "Dry Cardrona", you may ask? The saying arose from a much earlier event in 1877, on "the day they drank the pub dry". As the story goes, "Joe was a tunneller who was known to have rich relations in Great Britain. One day in 1877 a trooper rode over the Roaring Meg Track on the Pisa Range and asked for Joe, an incident that gave rise to rumours that Joe had inherited 500 pounds. By the end of the week the rumoured amount had grown to 500,000 pounds and that Saturday night Joe and his newfound 'friends' (by now most

Paddy Galvin's restored mudbrick cottage, 2005

of the town) drank the town dry. All on credit in anticipation of Joe receiving the money. Slowly the truth dawned when Joe was seen to be deputy returning officer at the local polling booth. The trooper had simply been delivering Joe's appointment notice!"

Today Cardrona is experiencing a new 'gold' rush, tourism and skiing. The skifield on Mt Cardrona and the Nordic cross-country skiing on Mt Pisa. But as you drive along the Cardrona Valley look for the gold workings

"Headquarters" of the Criffel Lead sluicing claim, Criffel Range. *Southland Museum*

Large sluiced basin on the summit of the Criffel Range. Holding dam in foreground and another one on the opposite side. Mt Pisa Range on skyline.

of yesteryear. These are particularly striking at the entrance to John Lee's Snow Farm, where the sculptured shapes of sluicings can readily be seen from the main highway.

The Criffel diggings

At the Wanaka end of the Pisa Range is Criffel Peak, which was named by surveyor James McKerrow after a town near his home in Scotland. Mt Pisa itself was named by J. T. Thomson because a huge leaning rock on its summit reminded him of the "leaning tower of Pisa".[3]

In 1885[4] it was reported that two enterprising prospectors from Cardrona, Wilson and Holloway, had discovered "rich auriferous ground" on the eastern summit slopes of the Criffel Range.

By the end of 1885 there were 50 miners on the diggings and 30 were on to payable gold. Out of the 1,000 ounces of gold extracted during the 1884-85 season, the discoverers Wilson and Holloway obtained 300 ounces.

In spite of these good returns Criffel never really thrived because of its high altitude (1,300 metres), which meant that as the winter snow approached the diggings had to close for several months. Also on the tops there was a lack of water to wash the pay-dirt. Some miners sledged their dirt across to Luggate Creek for washing, until Wilson and Holloway cut a water race from the creek to the diggings. Supplies were also a problem, but this was overcome when Robert McDougall of Cardrona brought them up by pack track and set up a branch store at Criffel.

Because of its seasonal nature and lack of water, Criffel never supported a large population and after a decade the diggings closed down.

REFERENCES.
1. Pyke, Vincent, *Early Gold Discoveries in Otago*, 1887.
2. Hassing, George, *Memory Log of G. M. Hassing*, 1929.
3. Hall-Jones, John, *John Turnbull Thomson*, 1992
4. Roxburgh, Irvine, *Wanaka Story*, 1977

CHAPTER 9
The Golden Arrow

*Came across Fox's party and about 40 others
quietly working in a secluded gorge of the Arrow River.*
Dr James Hector

Because of his early association with the rich gold in the Arrow River, William Fox came to be regarded as the original discoverer. Early Arrowtown became known as "Fox's" and even the centennial monument inside the entrance of the Arrow Gorge bears the inscription, "William Fox discovered gold near here in 1862".

The real discoverer of gold in the Arrow River was a Maori from Thames, Jack Tewa, better known as "Maori Jack", who worked at W. G. Rees' station at Queenstown Bay. Rees relates[1] how Maori Jack "showed him a sample of gold which he had washed with his shovel from the bed of the Arrow, early in August 1862". Next came John McGregor and his brother-in-law, Thomas Low, who were looking for pastoral land and visited Rees' station, where they learned from a cadet of Maori Jack's find. Late in September they "found gold in large quantities [in the Arrow Gorge] at the back of the present Arrowtown" and decided to stay on mining.

"McGregor and Low were getting at least 20 ounces of gold a day [only using] cradles", Rees informs us.[1] It was fully five days later that Fox arrived, but as Rees comments, "Fox like a fool must need go to the Dunstan [for supplies] and as a consequence he was watched and followed" in what became known as the great foxhunt. The first to hunt Fox down was an American by the name of West. Then in October Ben Bowman and Dan Sutherland discovered Fox's secret gorge, as John Cormack relates:[1]

"After prospecting the Arrow River where the Arrow Gorge comes out onto the flat (now the site of Arrowtown) Bowman and Sutherland examined the mouth of the gorge. They observed that the river extended from the cliff of one side to the other and concluded that no one was further up the river. Then while they were sitting on a knoll having a quiet smoke, they were intrigued to see two men wading down through the gorge up to their waists in water, each with a piece of rope in his hand. They then disappeared towards Lake Hayes. Two hours later they returned, each carrying a carcase of sheep on his back, waded into the river and disappeared up the gorge. Puzzled, Bowman and Sutherland returned to the gorge the next day and on wading about a quarter of a mile up through the gorge they came on McGregor and Low at their camp. They also met West and later Fox, who was much put out by the invasion of 'his' realm and said that he would have to tie them up to prevent them leaving and spreading the word. However, after West had

John McGregor, who was goldmining in the Arrow River with Thomas Low five days before William Fox arrived.
June Wood

Sketch of the 'canvas town' of Arrowtown at the beginning of the gold rush. Entrance to the Arrow Gorge on extreme right. *Illustrated London News*

Monument to William Fox's 'rediscovery' of the gold in the Arrow Gorge.

spoken (favourably) on their behalf, he relented and they were allowed to fetch their mate, Cormack, but under dire threats of punishment if they brought anyone else back."

All parties agreed to work on in secret and for a month "each party did well" as Cormack records:[1]

> "McGregor's party got 82 pounds weight in gold.
> Fox's party got 40 pounds weight in 2 weeks.
> We, the 'New Chum, party, got 110 pounds weight in 4 weeks, three days.
> We cradled 109 ounces of gold in one day."

The figures were sensational and exceeded Hartley and Reilly's 87 pounds weight of gold in the Dunstan rush.

By now there were about 30 diggers in the hidden valley in the gorge, all under the leadership of Fox. Fox was 'elected' as 'commissioner' and he proceeded to make his own 'laws' for the goldfield. Each man was allowed 60 foot of frontage to the river and the penalty for 'jumping' a claim was to fight Fox! Small wonder that the original mining settlement at Arrowtown became known as "Fox's".

The old Arrowtown gaol today.

For over a month Fox reigned supreme in the hidden valley. Then came the visit of the provincial geologist, Dr James Hector[1], who after following up the Cardrona Valley and crossing the Crown Range "came upon Fox's party and about forty others quietly working in a secluded gorge of the Arrow River". A few days after Dr Hector's visit "a large party of miners pursuing nearly the same track, observed the smoke of camp fires and following this clue they suddenly presented themselves on the scene of operations." The 'foxhunt' was over, the wily Fox had been tracked down to his lair.

Miners poured into the narrow confines of the gorge, where confusion reigned on the greatly restricted terrace. Whereas the original diggers were prepared to reduce their huge claims down to the legal size of 24 square feet, the newcomers soon noticed that there was a certain amount of 'peg changing' going on. "A mob of Tipperary men were going about and jumping portions of the richest claims."[2] The mood was ugly and some of the claim-holders set off in haste to Dunstan to apply for an injunction. But the commissioner at Dunstan found that his appointment did not extend to the Arrow, so Sergeant-Major Bracken of the mounted police was sent to maintain law and order and to try and settle the claim disputes. Bracken had earlier distinguished himself in arresting the two robbers, Kelly and Burgess and was highly respected among the mining community.

When Bracken arrived at the Arrow he found everything in disorder, with men defending their claims armed with revolvers. He addressed the men: "Look here diggers, I have been sent up here to enforce order and by God I will."[2] As he spoke his fingers toyed with his pistol and the miners who knew of him listened with respect. The best way to settle the claim disputes, he pronounced, was for the miners to appoint two disinterested men as assessors in each case and he would act as arbitrator. This was agreed to at once and Bracken proceeded to read out the regulations dealing with the subject. The noisy Tipperary men were so astounded that they could only look on, speechless. Then Bracken proceeded to settle the disputes by getting the miners to appoint disinterested assessors and after explaining the by-laws to them they made their own decision. This simple procedure gave great satisfaction and avoided bloodshed.

By 23 December 1862 there were '1,500' men camped at the Arrow and the embryo 'canvastown' of Arrowtown had formed at the entrance to the gorge.

Macetown

By late 1862 prospectors were working their way up the narrow Arrow Gorge. Out in front were the Mace brothers from Yorkshire, John, Christopher ("Kit"), Charles and Henry ("Harry"),[3] who were already well known as cricketers. Nine miles up the brothers burst out of the gorge to a wide open valley with terraces and river flats. Continuing over the terraces they came to a creek entering the Arrow from the west and they staked their claim at the junction. The creek being 12 miles up from Arrowtown they called it Twelve Mile Creek (now the Rich Burn).

Meantime, two other brothers from

Approaching the wooded terrace of Macetown today. Arrow River in foreground, Advance Peak on skyline.

England, John and Joseph ("Joe") Beale[3], had come over the hills from Skippers (see next chapter) and followed the Twelve Mile Creek down to the terraces (later the site of Macetown), where they pitched their tent. Next morning John Beale went down to the creek to fetch a billy of water and spotting some gold in the creek he filled a pannikin with it. Returning to their tent he noticed some men (the Mace brothers) pitching their tent on the opposite side of the Arrow River. The two parties met and coming to an

Houses of the "Twelve Apostles", Macetown.
Lakes District Museum

The Golden Arrow 105

An early photograph of High Street, Macetown.
Lakes District Museum

Right: The same view today.

amicable arrangement they worked their separate claims, near to each other.

Soon, other miners were pouring into the valley from all directions (Skippers, Wanaka via the Motatapu Saddle, the Cardrona via Brackens Gully, as well as the Arrow Gorge). A township sprang up on the terraces and this was given the name of Twelve Mile, because of its close proximity to Twelve Mile Creek. The Mace brothers erected a large store in the town and it was only after they left in 1865 for the West Coast gold rush that the town was renamed Macetown in their honour.

Because of the narrow confines of the river terrace, the town straggled nearly a mile along the one main street, High Street. There were two principal hotels in the town, the Macetown Hotel and almost opposite, the Alpine Hotel. The Mace brothers' store served as a post office until one was built in 1865. A school was built in 1870 and later a public hall.

Because of its harsh, snow-bound winters, the population of Macetown was never huge, peaking at 300 in 1863 (far less than some wild guesses). This dropped off with the start of the West Coast gold rush in 1865. As the Europeans shifted away Chinese miners moved in to rework the abandoned claims. When the Rich Burn reefs were opened up in 1876, the population received a boost and for many years 150-200 people lived in and around Macetown, although many retreated to Arrowtown as winter approached.

On the northern outskirts of the town were the huts of the "Twelve Apostles", a name which was bestowed only because of their number.

The Twelve Apostles were a group of happy-go-lucky miners who banded together to

Tylie Smith's bakery in autumn colours.
J. R. White

drink and gamble. When the cash ran out they went back to work to earn enough money to repeat the cycle. The best known "Apostle" was "Doc" McKenzie who lived on a terrace, slightly 'superior' to the others, in a stone hut which he kept spotlessly clean. "Doc" was famous for finding the largest nugget ever recovered from the Arrow River. Weighing 16 ounces, he found it in the river just below the cemetery. Doubtless he gambled it away in their gambling den, which they called "Montezuma". In spite of their sessions of boozing all twelve "Apostles" reached their allotted age of "three scores years and ten".

One of the stalwarts of Macetown was William ("Tylie") Smith,[3] an Englishman, who arrived in 1863 and opened a store in partnership with Robert McDougall of Cardrona. Tylie Smith also built a stone bakehouse at the back of the store, where he employed a German baker by the name of Sneider. He also employed a Chinaman, Ah Wak, to drive a cart to and from Arrowtown for supplies and for the mail, when it was "Mr Smith's month for the contract". In 1919 Tylie Smith suffered a serious head injury while driving down to Arrowtown and after his long residence in Macetown he closed his store and bakery and moved to Christchurch, where he died in 1924 aged 91. His store, which was built of corrugated iron, was dismantled for use elsewhere, but his stone bakery has survived and has recently been restored by DOC.

Stone cottage of schoolteacher Joseph Needham, who taught at Macetown school for ten years.

"Billy" Jenkins, the last inhabitant and self-proclaimed 'Mayor' of Macetown. *Alexander Turnbull Library*

The other intact building at Macetown belonged to Joseph Needham, an ex-miner turned school teacher, who taught at the Macetown school for ten years (1879-1889), the longest serving teacher at the school. Needham's stone cottage has also been restored by DOC. The recollections of a child at Macetown school have been beautifully told by Josephine Traill in her charming little book, *Child of the Arrow*, (1984).

A wooden building of unknown ownership was recently destroyed by fire, by a tramper using it for shelter.

The last inhabitant of Macetown was William Jenkins ("Billy Jenks"), whose widowed mother ran the Alpine Hotel. In his latter years Billy Jenks became the sole 'citizen' of the town, with the self-proclaimed title of the "Mayor of Macetown". 'Mayor Jenks' died in 1945.

Today, thanks to the townsfolk who planted many deciduous trees, the site of Macetown has matured into a beautiful woodlands park, which is particularly colourful in the autumn. In the spring daffodils are in bloom.

THE RICH BURN REEFS

Gold-bearing quartz reefs were discovered in the Rich Burn Valley as early as 1863, but these were not developed while the easier alluvial mining was still payable. Macetown's poor access was also a major hindrance to development, the cost of bringing in heavy machinery being prohibitive. Then in 1875 the provincial government offered a pound-for-pound subsidy[4] for successful prospecting of quartz reefs, sparking off quartz mining.

In 1876 quartz reef mining began in the Rich Burn Valley, the Tipperary and Premier mines being the most successful. Over a period of nearly 40 years from 1876 until 1914, when the last mine closed down, a total

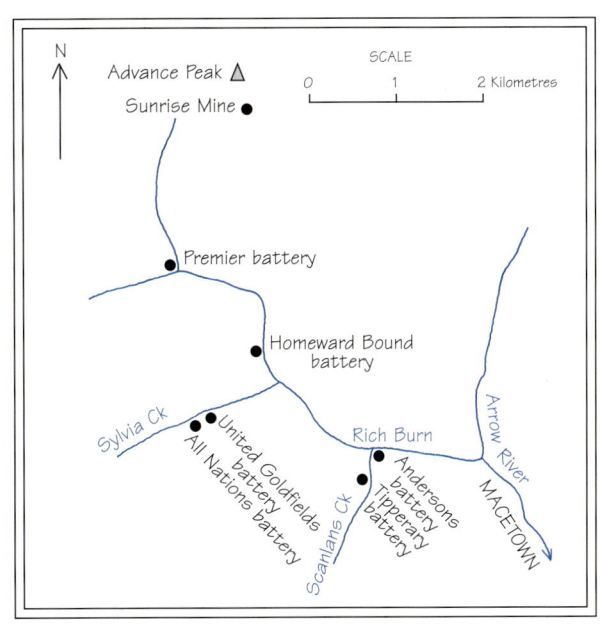

Sketch map of the Rich Burn gold batteries.
Copyright J. Hall-Jones

The Anderson brothers' battery. Note unusual iron frame.

Tipperary battery c.1900. Battery shed on right, furnace under the shelter on left. *Lakes District Museum*

of 50,000 ounces of gold was recovered from the reefs. Of this, 26,000 ounces came from the Premier mine and 20,000 ounces from the Tipperary mine. All the other mines accounted for a total of only 5,000-10,000 ounces.

Starting from the carpark at the end of the road from Macetown and heading up the Rich Burn Valley, the mines and their quartz crushing batteries are as follows:

Andersons battery

Situated the carpark, the ten stamp Andersons battery was erected by the Anderson brothers, James and William[3], identical twins from Scotland and their brother-in-law, William Hannah. An iron-framed battery, it was the only one of its kind in Otago[4.] The associated berdan for fine crushing stands close by.

Tipperary battery

Up Scanlans Creek from Andersons battery there were several mines (including Andersons) of which the Tipperary mine was one of the most productive of the Macetown reefs. The ten stamp Tipperary battery was erected in 1879, about 500 metres up Scanlans Creek from its junction with the Rich Burn. A furnace was also constructed at the battery to fire the concentrates after crushing, to increase the gold takings.[4] Unfortunately severe floods in 1999 badly damaged the battery site and no machinery remains. The stone furnace is still partly standing.

Sylvia Creek batteries

Continue up the Rich Burn to its Sylvia Creek branch, where there were two batteries, the All Nations and United Goldfields. The All Nations is described in 1878 as a "four stamper battery, very compact", as can be seen in a photograph in 1897.

The United Goldfields battery was constructed in 1910 from parts of the All Nations and other batteries to rework their mines. Although now decrepit, this ten stamp battery is still standing.

Homeward bound batteries

Dubbed the "giant coffee grinder" because of its shape and size, the huge Homeward Bound battery stands on the bank of the Rich Burn, a little above the Sylvia Creek junction. It was the third and largest of a series to be built by the Homeward Bound Co. The original battery, the first one at Macetown, was erected in 1876, but it was too small to crush the quartz. A second larger battery was constructed, only to be destroyed by a disastrous slip. The third and last

The Golden Arrow

Homeward Bound battery was built from the old Otago Pioneer Quartz (OPQ) battery at Waipori (see chapter 2), which was purchased, dismantled and re-erected on the Rich Burn. A ten stamp battery, it operated until the outbreak of war in 1914, when the British backers of the company ceased all funding and the battery closed down.

The third Homeward Bound battery, before it was roofed over. *J. R. White*

The ten stamps of the Homeward Bound battery were manufactured in England. Note stamps set at different levels for continuous crushing of the quartz in the stamper box.

The "very compact" All Nations battery, c.1897. *Burton Bros.*

The collapsing United Goldfields battery, 2005.

Rotting wooden frames of the Premier battery, 1979.

One of the cyanide vats of the Premier battery, 1979.

Premier battery

Continue up the Rich Burn track from the Homeward Bound battery until the Premier battery is reached Originally, erected as a five stamp battery by the Maryborough Co. in 1876, the battery did not do well and the company went into liquidation.

The neighbouring Premier mine purchased the plant and increased the number of stamps to ten and later twenty. In 1893 the Premier mine installed a cyanide plant to further extract the gold after crushing, one of the first in New Zealand to do so. The Premier mine became the most successful of the Rich Burn mines and continued until 1905 when it closed down. Today, the derelict Premier battery is still standing, with two wooden cyanide vats close by.

Advance Peak

There were a number of mines high on Advance Peak, the Sunrise mine at 5,500 feet being "the highest gold mine in the country".[5] The ore was conveyed down to the Premier battery for crushing, but with high operating costs and exposed working conditions on the bleak mountainside, most of the mines soon closed down.

During the late 1930s a small two stamp battery, driven by a petrol engine, operated on Advance Peak, the highest gold battery in New Zealand.[4] It remained there until removed illegally some years ago.

William Scoles' diversion tunnel in the Arrow Gorge.

Rev. George McNeur visits two Chinese miners at their stone hut near Arrow Falls, 1901. *Alexander Turnbull Library*

For further information on the gold mines of the Rich Burn, Peter Petchey's excellent *Archaeological Survey of the Arrow River and Macetown* (2002) is strongly recommended.

Road to Macetown

Macetown's poor access via the narrow gorge was a major problem. In winter, when the town became snowbound and the Arrow River froze, Macetown was virtually isolated. A pack track led up the gorge and although horses' shoes were sharpened and pointed frost nails were fitted to grip the ice, pack train work was hazardous. A pack track was constructed over Big Hill as an alternative route to the gorge, but this was steep and extremely dangerous in the ice and snow of winter. In 1880 the people of Macetown began to petition for a proper road up the river route. A belated start was made on the road in 1881, but it was not until 1884 that the 15 kilometre road was constructed up the river, albeit with 23 crossings on the way.

Today it is very much a 4WD road or, alternatively, an interesting tramp with relics of the goldmining days of yesteryear along the way. The Department of Conservation has an excellent route guide available, with points of interest marked by numbered posts along the road. Some of the highlights include the stone monument at the beginning of the gorge, with the plaque commemorating the 'discovery' of the gold by William Fox in 1862. At Brittania Terrace (where the Rule Britannia Sluicing Co. worked) look down at Scoles tunnel in the river, where in 1887 William Scoles drove a tunnel through a razor-back ridge to divert the river, only to find that the bared riverbed had already been worked.

As you cross Brackens Gully think of the early miners who used this as a route to the diggings from Wanaka and Cardrona. Brackens Gully was not named after the brave Sergeant-Major Bracken who restored order at the diggings, but after Christopher Bracken, an early miner in the gully. As you continue on, look across at Hayes Creek for the tailings and water races of the Shamrock sluicing claim on Big Hill, which worked from

Chinese huts and market gardens on the bank of Bush Creek, Arrowtown, c.1900. Ah Lum's store in the distance.
Lakes District Museum

Left: Renovated Ah Lum's store, 2005.

1910 to 1914. The old sledge track to this claim branches off the road further on. Nearing Eight Mile Creek are the remains of Mt Soho station homestead, the station's hut and the suspension bridge for stock. At Eight Mile Creek the Big Hill track descends to join the road, a popular alternative tramping route to Macetown, with great views and dry feet! From Nine Mile Creek you gain your first view of the terraces of Macetown, with the summit of Advance Peak high above.

Arrowtown's Chinatown

Nowadays, Arrowtown is a charming little town with many historic buildings and tall popular trees that turn golden in the autumn. Two highlights of a visit to the town are the Lakes District Museum, with its excellent displays and the historic Chinatown, which in 1953 was excavated by archaeologists and reconstructed as a model Chinese settlement.

The settlement was on the bank of Bush Creek, where it bubbles into the Arrow River at the north end of Arrowtown. Here the Chinese lived in their tiny huts of stone or mudbrick, while others dwelt in caves on the rocky hillside behind. There were three stores at the settlement, of which Ah Lum's stone store still stands and only the stone privy of Ah Wak's store survives. An earlier wooden store, owned by Su Sing, was a very long and narrow building and as such was known as the "Long House". In its heyday the Long House was the hub of the little community, serving as both a store and a social hall. It is described in 1870 as being surrounded by "20 comfortable sod huts". Just how many Chinese lived permanently in these huts is unknown. Some would be working in the extensive market gardens at the settlement, while others would be using it as a retreat from their mines in the Arrow Gorge and Macetown during the harsh winter months.

Mary Romans[6] remembers Ah Lum as a "distinguished looking person, elegant, immaculate, a personality who drew everybody's respect. He was well versed in English and acted as interpreter for his less fortunate kinsmen, wrote their letters and attended to their banking and other business." On Saturdays, vegetables from the market gardens at the settlement were paraded through Arrowtown, with Ah Lum out in front. "Ah Lum was taller than his followers and usually walked with his arms folded high across his chest and wearing a long smocklike garment, embroidered round the hemline. He wore a small green cap with a tassel, with his splendid pig tail hanging down behind. Following was a procession of up to 30 Chinese walking two abreast and carrying their ginger jars on sticks hung across their shoulders, while others carried lanterns." Mary Romans also recalls the thrilling experience of being sent to Ah Lum's store to buy something. "The Chinese would be sitting on the floor and they treated Ah Lum like a king."

Ah Lum acquired his stone store from Loo Lee in 1909 and died there in 1927. In front of Ah Lum's store was the one belonging to Ah Wak, who carted supplies to Tylie Smith's shop at Macetown. In 1905 Ah Wak's store was burnt down, only the stone privy surviving.

During 1983 Neville Ritchie[7] and a team of archaeological students excavated the area, unearthing the sites of eleven stone and mudbrick huts. In one hut the team found the remains of opium tins and smoking equipment and concluded that it was the social centre of the little community. No firm evidence of Su Sing's Long House was found, probably because of the subsequent market

"Old Tom's" hut restored, 1986.

Surviving stone privy of Ah Wak's store, 1986.

Restored Chinese stone hut, 1986. Note typical rounded chimney beside doorway at one end of the hut.

gardening of the site. During 1985-86 considerable conservation work was done on Ah Lum's store and since then some of the Chinese huts have been reconstructed, making a visit to Arrowtown's Chinatown a fascinating and instructive experience.

REFERENCES
1. Pyke, Vincent, *Early Gold Discoveries in Otago*, 1887
2. Gilkison, Robert, *Early Days in Central Otago*, 1930.
3. Beaton, Eileen, *Macetown*, 1971
4. Petchey, Peter *Archaeological Survey of the Arrow River and Macetown*, 2002.
5. Veitch, A. J., *Macetown*, 1972, unpub.
6. Romans, Mary, *Southland Times*, 1988.
7. *Southland Times*, 1983.

CHAPTER 10
The Richest River in the World

*It was the largest rush
that ever occurred in Otago.*
Vincent Pyke, 1887

Arthur of Arthurs Point

The story of Thomas Arthur and Harry Redfern who discovered the gold at Arthurs Point on the Shotover River is a classic 'rags to riches' tale.[1] Arthur and Redfern had been engaged to shear William Rees' flock at his station at Queenstown Bay. Arriving by boat at Queenstown Bay with his trousers in tatters, Arthur was embarrassed to learn that there were women ashore. He refused to leave the boat until an intact pair was produced.

In November 1862, on their first Sunday off, the two shearers strolled across to the point (Arthurs Point) where the Edith Cavell bridge now spans the Shotover River. There on the beach "Arthur washed out four ounces of gold with his tin dish in three hours".[2] Ecstatic, they hurried back to the station where Rees, seeing that it was hopeless to try and retain them, generously provided, flour, tea and sugar and let them go.

So rich was Arthurs Point that Arthur and his three mates won 200 ounces of gold in eight days. A visitor to Arthur's tent in

Queenstown Bay, 1864. A very early painting of Queenstown by J. T. Thomson. *Hall-Jones family.*

November was shown a dish full of gold lying under his stretcher.[2] Unlike Fox they made no secret of their discovery and soon the Shotover River was swarming with miners in the largest rush that ever occurred in Otago.[2] Many struck it rich and the miners soon referred to the Shotover River as the "richest river in the world". (The Shotover River was named by Rees after Shotover House, Oxford, the residence of one of his partners, George Maitland.)[3]

Thomas Arthur *after* he discovered the gold at Arthurs Point.
Lakes District Museum

The Maori of Maori Point

Undaunted by the gorge beyond Arthurs Point prospectors traversed the lofty mountains that hemmed in the "golden river" and descended to the beaches wherever a break occurred in its rocky margins. One of the most remarkable discoveries of gold was at Maori Point (as it became known) by two Maori from the North Island, Dan Ellison (Raniera Erihana) and Hakaria Maeroa. Vincent Pyke visited Hakaria (at Otago Heads), whose story of their discovery was interpreted for him:[3]

"As Dan and Hakaria, with other miners, were travelling along the eastern bank of the river, they found some Europeans working with great success

Left: Dan Ellison (Raniera Erihana) one of the two Maori who discovered the gold at Maori Point.
Lakes District Museum

The bank and gold office at Maori Point, 1864. Bank manager G. M. Ross in doorway, police sergeant on left.
Alexander Turnbull Library

John Aspinall's sluicing claim at Skippers Point. Miles Aspinall on right. *Lakes District Museum*

in a secluded gorge. On the opposite shore was a wide beach of unusually promising appearance, occupying a bend of the stream, over which the rocky cliffs rose perpendicularly to the height of more than 500 feet. Tempting as this spot was to the practised eyes of the miners, none of them would venture to breast the impetuous torrent. The Maoris, however, boldly plunged into the river, and succeeded in reaching the western bank; but a favourite dog that had followed them was carried away by the current, and drifted down to a rocky point, where it remained. Dan went to its assistance, and observing some particles of gold in the crevices of the rocks, he examined the sandy beach beneath, from which, with the aid of Hakaria, he gathered twenty-five pounds weight – 300 ounces – of the precious metal before nightfall."

With such an incredibly rich find, a town, Charlestown, sprang up almost overnight on the flat land of Maori Point. With riches being won daily from the beaches, Charlestown was alive with excitement and activity. There were at least seven shanty hotels, five stores, two butchers, a baker, a post office and a bank at the township. There was also a police station with a sergeant and a constable, and a resident magistrate who was appointed to settle claim disputes quickly on location. For a short time Charlestown thrived, peaking with a population over 1,000. But by 1864 the easily gained gold had been won and the population of the area dropped to about 400. Gradually businesses closed down and people drifted away. Today, no sign of Charlestown remains, only a small plaque which marks the site.

Skippers

The origin of the wellknown name, Skippers, remained a mystery until Peter Chandler,[7] the authority on the area, concluded that it was named after "Skipper" Malcolm Duncan, who discovered gold

"Skipper" Malcolm Duncan of Skippers Point. *Cyclopedia of NZ*

Skippers Pt

Facing page, above: Skippers Point settlement c.1890. Skippers Hall on the extreme right. John Aspinall's house in the trees in the distance. *Lakes District Museum*

Facing page, below: Skippers Point c.1891, showing the Skippers Sluicing Co's basin below Mt Aurum homestead and Skippers school. The second Skippers bridge in foreground. *Lakes District Museum*

there in 1862. Born in Northern Ireland, Duncan served for a number of years in American ships, hence his nickname of "Skipper". In 1857 he left the sea to work on the gold diggings in Australia and in 1861 he ventured across to Gabriels Gully. In 1862 he took part in the rush to the Shotover River, where he discovered gold at the junction of the river with a tributary (Skippers Creek), which soon became known as Skippers Point or just plain "Skippers".

One of the earliest to take advantage of Skipper Duncan's discovery was John Aspinall,[1] a Lancastrian who arrived in Queenstown in 1862. Following up the west bank of the Shotover River Aspinall began prospecting at Skippers Point. The returns were so good that he sent for his brother, William, in Australia and they tunnelled the claim together. After two years William had 'made his pile' and returned home to Lancashire, while John settled at his claim at Skippers Point, where he cut in water races and began to sluice in 1872.

H. A. Gordon, the Inspector of Mines in New Zealand, visited John Aspinall in 1887 and was most impressed with what he saw. "Aspinall was the first to take up a lease at Skippers Point", writes Gordon in his report to Parliament.[4] "He later bought out one claim after another and now holds the whole of the auriferous ground (ten acres) at Skippers Point, from which he has taken about 30,000 pounds worth of gold. He is one of the most enterprising miners in the colony", continues Gordon, "and has the most improved hydraulic appliances for working his claim, all manufactured by himself on the ground. Indeed his workshop and tools, although he lays no claim to be a mechanic, would not disgrace some engineering establishments."

John Aspinall and his wife, Elizabeth, lived in their large two-storeyed house above the claim and here they raised their family of nine children. Aspinall died in 1890 but the family carried on working the claim until 1918, when it was taken over.

Other claims were taken up on the gold-bearing terraces on the west side of the Shotover River between Skippers Point and Maori Point, where the remains of their water races, holding dams, sluicings and tailings are still obvious today. Next to Aspinall's claim is the huge sluiced basin of the Skippers Sluicing Co's claim, below Mt Aurum station's homestead and Skippers School (both recently restored by DOC).

With all this mining activity at Skippers Point and along the golden terraces there was an initial population of about 1,000,[1] but by 1864 it has stabilised to about 200. At one stage there were six hotels at Skippers Point, but like Maori Point their life was short.

The one hotel that survived for many years was the Otago Hotel, owned by Samuel

The Otago Hotel at Skippers Point. John Flynn leaning against buggy and his wife, Rachael, standing beside doorway. *Lakes District Museum*

Ruins of the Otago Hotel, 1979.

Johnston. Johnston's Otago Hotel offered accommodation, a dining room and a billiard room and served as the social centre for the Skippers community. It also contained the Skippers post office and a bakery business. Next door to the hotel was a little corrugated iron building which housed the only public telephone at Skippers. Samuel Johnston died in 1896[1] but his wife, Eliza, carried on the hotel until 1908 when her son-in-law, John Flynn, took over the licence until it lapsed in 1919. Thus the Johnston family owned the hotel for almost 60 years, the entire life of the business. The hotel was eventually bought by Archie Macnicol, owner of Mt Aurum station, who removed the wooden part of the building, leaving the stone portion and these are the remains seen today.

There was also a public hall at Skippers Point, built by public subscription, where dances and concerts were held. For a short time there was a police station at Skippers, manned by two constables, but after a year this closed down.

Today the cemetery at Skippers contains some interesting headstones including those of Samuel and Eliza Johnston and the successful miner John Aspinall and his wife, Elizabeth. Also Koo Hoy Yow, a Chinese miner who "died from an accidental fall in 1904".[5] Of more recent times is the delightful inscription on the grave of Lorraine Borrell

Koo Hoy Yow's headstone in Skippers cemetery.

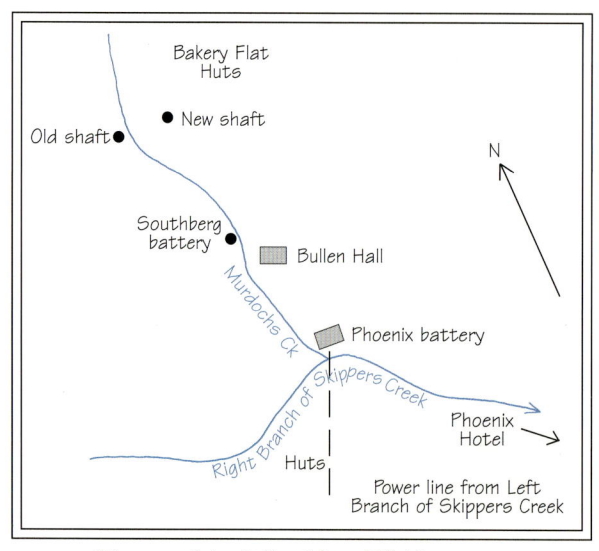

of The Branches station, further up the Shotover River:

> "My time is up, I've been clocked out.
> The judge has tapped the gavel.
> I'll retire the teapot, lay the knitting down
> and quietly unravel."

Bullendale

The rich deposits of alluvial gold at Skippers Point suggested that there was a rich mother lode further up Skippers Creek. But no reef was found until floods in the early spring of 1863 caused a slip, baring a quartz outcrop which was discovered by a Norwegian prospector, Alex Olsen.[1] The reef was near the head of the right branch of Skippers Creek, where a sample returned one ounce of gold from one bucket of stone. Rightly Olsen's reef became known as the "Scandinavian Reef".

Olsen's discovery led to the realisation that there were other sources of gold in the area as distinct from alluvial. Many claims were pegged off and quartz mining companies were formed with a view to raising money to erect crushing batteries. Most of these

Diagram of the Bullendale goldfield.
Copyright J. Hall-Jones

Above, top: The Phoenix 30 stamp battery at Bullendale. The rockcrusher is to the right of the top of the smoke stack. *Lakes District Museum*

Above: Closer view of the rockcrusher, 1979.

Right: From the top of the Bullendale battery looking across at part of the Bullendale settlement on the hillside opposite. In the foreground, Murdochs Creek and the track to the mines and Bakery Flat. *Otago Settlers Museum*

Goldfields of Otago

Poppet head of the
original Bullendale mine.
Lakes District Museum

companies were merely speculative and once it dawned that the only access to the claims was a rough pack track over 30 kilometres long the majority pulled out. Only two companies survived, the Great Scandinavian, which in 1866 erected the 30 stamper Phoenix battery at the confluence of Skippers and Murdochs Creeks, and the Otago, which in 1867 erected the 16 stamper Southberg battery in Murdochs Creek, upstream from the Phoenix battery. (Southberg and Murdoch were both pioneer prospectors in the area and major shareholders in the Otago company.)

With the Great Scandinavian Co. came George Bullen, a merchant and principal shareholder, who was to buy out the company and become the owner of the Phoenix battery. Later he acquired the Southberg's ground from the Otago Co, leaving him the sole owner of the whole goldfield. Bullen was to invest a considerable amount of money in working this field, including the building of Bullen Hall as a recreational centre for the miners and their families. Deservedly the mining settlement on the goldfield became known as "Bullendale".

As part of his development of the Phoenix mine, Bullen advertised in Australia for an experienced mine manager, with the result that Frederick Evans, an experienced Cornish miner, was appointed and was to manage the mine for the next 30 years. However, the arrival of Evans did not automatically mean immediate success. His two main problems were the lack of sufficient water to drive the huge 30 stamper battery, and the lack of payable stone. The latter was solved in 1884 when a new shaft was sunk and good stone was found some 50 metres lower than any previous workings. In February 1886 after a long time in the doldrums, the Phoenix mine returned 1,400 ounces of gold.

But the good news had a twist to it. The new deeper shaft required more powerful winding gear and extra pumping machinery,

Winding house of the new main shaft (note absence of poppet head). Fenced Bakery Flat above. *Hocken Library*

so more power was needed. Water power was unreliable because of a poor water supply and steam power had its drawbacks because of a scarcity of fuel. Electricity was the answer.

New Zealand's First Power Scheme

In 1884 Walter Prince[3] of Dunedin visited Bullendale to advise on the construction of what became the first hydro-electric power scheme in New Zealand. Prince recommended that a generating station be established at the foot of an 80 metre cliff in the left branch of Skippers Creek, so that a good head of water could be piped directly down onto two Pelton wheels which would in turn rotate two dynamos in the powerhouse. The current generated would be transmitted by No. 8 copper wire for about three kilometres over a spur to a motor in the battery shed which would drive the stamps.

Anyone who has trekked the seven kilometre gorge of Skippers Creek can appreciate the problems of packing in all the heavy machinery to the hydro-electric power station. Nevertheless by 3 February 1886 the two Pelton wheels and two dynamos were installed in the powerhouse at "Dynamo Flat" and the motor in the battery shed at Bullendale, ready for a trial test. Being New Zealand's first hydro-electric power scheme there were of course teething problems, including the discovery that the working of the second dynamo didn't simply double the power, as had been expected. As the inspector at that time commented, "very little is yet really known about electricity".[6] Nevertheless the system worked and as well as driving the battery and the gear at the mine there was a surplus of power to light Bullen Hall.

When the inspector of miners, H. A. Gordon,[4] visited Bullendale in 1887 he found that the system was working satisfactorily. "It being the first crushing battery driven by electricity there is great interest in the mining community", he comments. At the time of Gordon's visit there were "78 men" employed

Dynamo shed and penstocks of the power house at Dynamo Flat, the first hydro-electric power station in New Zealand. *Lakes District Museum*

One of the two dynamos at Dynamo Flat, 1979.

at the mine and a "rock-breaking machine" was being installed to pulverize the quartz as it is taken from the mine. This pulverized stone is then fed into the stamps of the crushing battery by self-feeding hoppers. "It is only recently that this mine has shown signs of paying", records Gordon. "From February 1884 to November 1885, 6,400 ounces of gold have been taken from the mine, while the total product is about 15,500 ounces."[4]

In 1893 Bullen sold his Phoenix mine to Achilles Goldfields Ltd who rebuilt the battery. However, by the end of the century most of the accessible gold had been recovered and the mine closed down in 1901. It was reopened briefly in 1904, but closed down permanently in 1905. Throughout its life of 40 years some good returns were made, the overall production probably exceeding 35,000 ounces.[1] However the expenses of operating a large quartz mine in such a rugged and remote area outweighed the returns and few people really benefited from the mine.

Bullendale Today

Peter Petchey in his excellent *Archaeological Survey of Bullendale* (1996)[6] gives a detailed inventory of what can be seen at the Bullendale mine today. To reach Bullendale from Skippers the tramper must resign himself to multiple criss-crossings of Skippers Creek with a climb out onto the old Bullendale Road at Roaring Meg Creek to negotiate this difficult gorge. The approach to the remains of the Phoenix battery at the junction of Murdochs Creek and the right branch of Skippers Creek is heralded by large pieces of rusting iron machinery that have been washed down Skippers Creek. The site of the battery house itself is a regular 'junkyard' of iron works, a challenging puzzle for a mining engineer, all carefully listed by Petchey.[6] Perched precariously on a spur above the battery is the rock crusher that was used to pulverise the stone from the mine before it was conveyed by self-feeding hoppers down to the battery of 30 stamps.

Behind the battery a track (now heavily overgrown with saplings) leads up through the forest on the true left bank of Murdochs Creek to a tussock flat, "Bakery Flat", where there are the remains of some of the Bullendale miners' huts and the oven of Cotter's bakehouse. About 200 metres from the start of this track are heaps of red bricks and two fireplaces, marking the site of Bullen Hall. On the opposite side of the creek from

Bullen Hall are some rusting relics from the Southberg battery.[6] Continuing up the track from Bullen Hall to just below Bakery Flat are some pieces of machinery from the winding house[6] of the new main shaft of 1896. As Petchey explains this shaft was on an incline so did not have the 'classic' poppet head of other mine shafts. On the other hand the older shaft on the opposite side of Murdochs Creek from here, was a vertical one which had the poppet head as shown in early photographs of the Bullendale mine.

Entirely separate from the Bakery Flat settlement, there was another group of miners' huts, on the sunny face opposite the battery where the transmission line crossed the spur from Dynamo Flat. On the bank of Skippers Creek below this part of the settlement was the popular Phoenix Hotel. Established in 1887 by Mrs Violet McArthur of McArthurs' Hotel in Long Gully, it was a centre for the miners to socialise, drink and play billiards. Phoenix Hotel was destroyed by fire in 1896, but was rebuilt by early 1897. Sited close to the edge of the creek it was subject to flooding and there is little to be seen of the old hotel today.

During the First World War the powerhouse in Dynamo Flat was dismantled and the machinery strewn about the site. To celebrate the centenary of this historic powerhouse in 1986 the two dynamos were partially restored and mounted on a platform of solid wooden beams.

Learning from the Bullendale's experience with hydro-electricity the Sandhills dredge in the upper Shotover River became the first electric dredge in New Zealand (see Chapter 13).

Other batteries

Although the Phoenix battery was the main quartz crushing battery in the Shotover basin there were other batteries working in the

Bricks and remains of one of the fireplaces of Bullen Hall, 2005.

Violet McArthur's Phoenix Hotel, on Skippers Creek below Bullendale.

The Nugget battery on the edge of the Shotover River. The mine and mining settlement directly above.
Lakes District Museum

area. Of these the most successful venture was the Nugget battery on the west bank of the Shotover River about two kilometres above the Skippers Creek junction. The battery was sited right on the river's edge and the quartz was trucked down for crushing from the mine directly above. An eight stamper battery, it returned a total 4,392 ounces of gold over a period of 11 years up to 1896.[1]

Two small batteries, the Crystal and the Leviathan worked in Sawyers Creek, up behind the Skippers cemetery. Both were four stamper batteries, having obtained their stamps from the disused Southberg battery at Bullendale.[6] Although both worked spasmodically from time to time neither were successful. Erected in a narrow creek bed, the Crystal battery has become badly damaged by repeated floods. The woodwork of the Leviathan battery has gradually rotted away making it difficult to find.

Archie Macnicol of Mt Aurum station had a small three stamper battery high in the Mt

The Richest River in the World

Aurum basin which he worked by water power in the summer months.

From pack track to road

With goldtowns springing up at Maori Point, Skippers and Bullendale there was an urgent need for a properly surveyed pack track to bring in supplies and machinery. In 1863 work began on a pack track from Arthurs Point to Maori Point which largely followed the current road to Skippers Saddle. It then dipped down Long Gully on the opposite side of today's road. From John and Violet McArthurs' Hotel at the bottom of Long Gully the track climbed steeply up to Green Gate Saddle to follow gently down the beautiful Green Gate Valley to Deep Creek, where the Green Gate Hotel was kept by Margaret Balderson[3] (known as "Green Gate Maggie"). After crossing Deep Creek the track led out to Maori Point. The line of this track is still obvious today and the keen tramper will find it a most rewarding walk, away from the noisy vehicles and hazards of the Skippers Road.

Archie Macnicol's three stamper battery in Mt Aurum basin. *J. R. White*

The Crystal battery in 1979. The battery has since become badly damaged by floods.

Remaining wooden frame of the Leviathan battery, 1979.

In 1866 the pack track was continued from Maori Point up the east bank of the Shotover River to opposite Londonderry Creek, where provincial engineer J. T. Thomson spanned the river with his remarkable suspension bridge, providing a safe crossing for the miners living at Skippers and Bullendale. Thomson's painting in 1868, two years after the erection of the bridge, shows a pack train heading up the steep side of the gorge to Skippers after crossing the bridge. (The foundations of the bridge can still be seen.) From Skippers the pack track to Bullendale followed the bed of Skippers Creek, criss-crossing along the way.

J. T. Thomson's original suspension bridge across the Shotover River at Skippers, 1866. Pack train heading up to Skippers township.
Hall-Jones family.

A carefully balanced load of sluice pipes on the narrow pack track to Skippers.
Lakes District Museum

The French-Canadian Julien Bourdeau who carried mail and stores to Skippers for over 40 years.

This narrow pack track remained the only formed access to the whole area for over 20 years. Then, as the easily won alluvial gold petered out there was an increasing demand for a proper road to bring in heavy sluice pipes and plant for the crushing batteries. For a time packers such as John Edgar and the redoubtable Julien Bourdeau were ingenious in the way they balanced the loads on their pack horses, but there was a limit to the weight they could carry.

The first positive move for a dray road to Skippers came in 1882 when John Aspinall of Skippers addressed the Lakes County

Bourdeau's stone store at the turn off of the current road to Coronet Peak. It is now a private house.
F. W. Craddock

Horse-drawn buggies rounding the notorious Pinchers Bluff on Skippers Road.
Hocken Library

The new Skippers bridge, with J. T. Thomson's original bridge far below. *P. C. Chandler*

Council on the need for a road. He subsequently backed this up with a petition signed by a large number of people at a public meeting at Skippers. After government approval, work commenced on the Skippers Road in 1883, but it was not until seven years later in 1890 that the narrow, tortuous 30 kilometre road to Skippers was completed.

One of the most difficult sections of the road was at Pinchers Bluff (named after the road engineer), where the road had to be blasted out of a sheer rock face 200 metres above the river. The task was a daunting one involving hand-drilling and explosives. Men were lowered on ropes to be suspended like flies on a wall as they drilled by hand into the rock face. The two McConochie brothers[1] were suspended on the face with ropes around their waists, when suddenly the whole rock mass began to move. To hesitate would be fatal and they literally ran up the moving face to safety!

The road in 1890 finished at J. T. Thomson's suspension bridge at Londonderry Creek. But the approaches to the bridge were very steep on both sides and no sooner had the road been completed than the clamour for a new higher bridge began. The site chosen for the new bridge was a spectacular one indeed. Upriver from the original low one, the new bridge would cross 100 metres above the river and would span a gorge with sheer rock faces on both sides. It was not a job for the faint-hearted! Work on the new bridge began in 1898 and took two years to complete. The official opening by the Minister of Mines on 29 March 1901 was a huge occasion, followed by a sumptuous banquet in Mrs Johnston's Otago Hotel and a ball in the Skippers Hall.

One casualty of the new road to Skippers was Violet McArthur's Hotel at the bottom of Long Gully on the old pack track. After the death of her husband, Violet McArthur sold out to Peter Bell and moved to Bullendale to take up the Phoenix Hotel. Bypassed by the new road, Bell shifted across to the other side of the gully and built a new hotel alongside the road. Unfortunately, Bell froze

The Welcome Home Hotel, Long Gully, on the road to Skippers. *Lakes District Museum*

Right: Two remaining chimneys of the Welcome Home Hotel, 2005.

to death in a water race after a fall from his horse. In 1908 his widow, Honora, sold out to Henry Lewis, whose family carried on the business until 1945, when the licence lapsed. Officially called the Welcome Home Hotel, it was always known to the locals as the Long Gully pub. Today two tall chimneys mark the site of this hotel which was a welcome stop for travellers on the challenging Skippers Road.

Moonlight and Moke Creek

From the Moonlight stables at Arthurs Point a well-graded track leads to the Moke Creek branch of the Shotover River and its tributary, Moonlight Creek.

In 1862 an Australian prospector, George Moonlight (not to be confused with the Australian bushranger Captain Moonlight), discovered gold in Moonlight Creek. There was an immediate rush to Moonlight and Moke Creeks, but the population soon settled down to a small permanent one based around Laughton and Gardiner's farm and store on the Moonlight Terrace. From the 1890s into the early 1900s the Moonlight Terraces were heavily sluiced in two large sluicing claims known as Moonlight No. 1 and Moonlight No. 2, the remains of which are still obvious.

At Moke Creek most of the mining was in

Moke Creek dredge at work, 1902. *Lakes District Museum*

the creek bed, where later, the Moke Creek dredge worked. One of the early storekeepers at Moke Creek was a Russian, Vasilio Seffer. His son, John Seffer, was the last inhabitant of 'Sefferstown', where his house is still standing. Below 'Sefferstown', above the junction of Moke and Moonlight Creeks, are

John Seffers' house at Sefferstown today.

Right: George Moonlight who discovered the gold at Moonlight in 1862. *P. May*

Remains of Moke Creek school, 1979.

the remains of the school that served the mining population of the two creeks.

Oxenbridge Tunnel

In 1906, when the easy alluvial gold in the Shotover River had become difficult to find, the Oxenbridge brothers had the bright idea of drilling a diversion tunnel through a rocky headland upriver from the Edith Cavell bridge, theorising that they would be able to work a dried up riverbed. It took three years to drill and blast the tunnel through the solid rock, only to find that they had miscalculated and that the level of the tunnel was over a metre too high! Undismayed, they corrected their error and proceeded to build a wing dam across the river, only to have it swept away by a reluctant river within one day of completion! Still undeterred they rebuilt the dam, only to find that they had to control the inevitable seepage with pumps driven by a steam engine. Having spent many thousands of pounds on the project they recovered only 600 pounds worth of gold. Nevertheless the Oxenbridge Tunnel serves as a fine memorial to the spirit and determination of the Oxenbridge family. It also provides an exciting finale to a white-water rafting trip down the Shotover River.

REFERENCES.
1 De La Mare, A. J., *The Shotover River*, 1993
2. Pyke, Vincent, *Early Gold Discoveries in Otago*, 1887
3. Chandler, Peter, *Let There Be Light*, 1986
4. Gordon, H. A., *Report on the Mining Industry in NZ*, 1887
5. Ng, James, *Windows on a Chinese Past*, 1995
6. Petchey, Peter, *Archaeological Survey of Bullendale*, 1996
7. Chandler, Peter, *pers.comm.*

White water cascading out of the Oxenbridge Tunnel. The steam engine was used for pumping out the bed of the Shotover River (behind).

CHAPTER 11
The Kawarau Dam

*I hope to see the Kawarau a hive of busy bees
with miners gathering the golden harvest.*
G. Cruickshank, 1924

By October 1867 the road through the Kawarau Gorge was completed and Cobb & Co. were running their coach service through to Queenstown from Dunedin three times a week. Initially the swift-flowing Kawarau River was crossed in two places by ferries, until these were replaced by bridges, the Victoria bridge (in 1878) and the historic Kawarau bridge (in 1880), from which bungy jumpers now leap.

These coach journeys to Queenstown were not without their hazards as Robert Gilkison records:[1]

> "There is a spot on the Kawarau which is called Parsons' Leap to this day. Tom Parsons was driving his four-horse coach, and crept slowly up the rise that leads where the road is cut round a bluff that is 200 ft above the river, and on the river side was a stone wall about two feet high ... As he rounded the bluff, some men who were at work on the road did something which startled the leaders, and they turned round and sprang over the wall, followed by the wheelers and the coach. The one passenger threw himself off, but Tom Parsons went with the coach, and was found on a little sandy place. The coach and horses were never seen more, being swept away by the river. Tom was broken wherever he could be, but was mended in time, and lived to drive another coach, but never by Parson's Leap."

The Kawarau Dam

In 1889 Sir Julius Vogel, one of New Zealand's early prime ministers, wrote a novel, *Anno Domini 2000*, in which the author and a 'Mr Fitzherbert' set about recovering the gold that must 'surely' be lying at the bottom of the Kawarau River.

In this imaginative novel,[2] the heroine became exceedingly rich through being a shareholder in a company which anticipated later gold seekers by making an opening in the glacial moraine at the southern end of Lake Wakatipu, thus enabling the lake to drain into the Mataura Valley. At the same time the company dammed the existing natural exit of the lake waters at the Kawarau Falls where the river leaves the lake. The book related that when the work was completed, thousands gathered along the banks of the Kawarau, and as the water gradually receded, a yellow colour was seen to appear more and more vividly. In one place a great cleft was exposed some twenty-seven feet long and five feet wide completely filled with the precious gold. Even with the use of only shovels and picks, gold to the value of over [2 million pounds] was extracted on the afternoon of the opening day of this fictitious bonanza.

Doubtless inspired by this piece of fiction, the Hon. G. M. Thomson resurrected the idea in 1919 with an address entitled "A Scientists's Daring Proposal",[2] in which he ponders over the problem of how to grasp the wealth of precious material that must 'undoubtedly' lie in the cracks and crevices at the bottom of the Clutha River. He then proposed that a national scheme for damming up the great lakes (Wakatipu, Wanaka and Hawea) which drain into the Clutha, could be profitably worked for the enrichment of the country. After this stirring address the usually staid and conservative *Otago Daily Times* went one step further. If it was solved successfully, it would go a long way towards paying New Zealand's national debt, it proclaimed.

And so the proposal to dam the outlet of Lake Wakatipu at Kawarau Falls was born and was to proceed. In 1924 the first shot was fired to blast the rock foundation for the

Kawarau Falls at the outlet of Lake Wakatipu. Robertson and Hallenstein's mill in foreground. Kawarau Falls station on far side. *Lakes District Museum*

dam. From the homely dais of the body of a motor truck, Warden George Cruickshank[2] outlined the dream of that far-seeing prophetic statesman, Sir Julius Vogel, whose novel also included the use of aircraft flying from Melbourne to Dunedin, to reach the Kawarau of his book. "He was right about the aircraft, so why might he not be right about the gold?", Cruickshank argued 'logically'. "This great sluice [the Kawarau] has been gathering gold for centuries, there must be millions [of ounces] there. I hope to see the Kawarau [bed] a hive of busy bees [miners] gathering the golden harvest."

By 30 August 1926 the dam had been completed and the great day arrived to close the ten gates. At 11 a.m. A. C. Hanlon, chairman of the Kawarau Company, authorised the official closure amid cheers from the crowd of 2,000 present. The spectators then hastened to all vantage points along the river, particularly in the gorge, to watch the 'drying up' process.

In preparation for collecting the "golden harvest" a special "gold coach" had been driven from Dunedin by a mechanic employed by the Kawarau Co. It was radically different from the gold escort coach of earlier days, being the very latest model single seater Ford, with a long back specially spot-welded for carrying the precious metal. The driver's task was, with an armed escort, to visit at set times the various claims, collect, weigh and seal up the bags of gold and transport them to the appointed bank.

But on the closing day the special correspondent reported that "a considerable trickle of water still found its way through below the gates and by 5 p.m. the river had just started to recede at Cromwell, 35 miles downstream. The river is still falling, but falling very slowly", he observed, "and it will have to drop many feet yet if there is to be any chance of winning payable gold". The next day he reviewed the situation with these ominous words:[2]

The official closure of the gates of the Kawarau Dam on 30 August 1926. *Courtesy Ron Murray*

Left: The Kawarau Dam with raised gates today.

"The cold facts of the Kawarau scheme have to be faced, however distasteful it may be to have to give them to the public. At half past eight this morning the water in the river at Cromwell had dropped three feet and at six o'clock tonight it had dropped only an inch or two more... The Kawarau scheme to lay bare the bed of the river has so far failed, and it seems hardly possible that the prospects can now be improved... The depth of the river which is at present flowing through the gorge goes to show without any shadow of doubt that the calculations of some people have been sadly astray."

Right: The Bell-Kilgour mine at Scotland Point, 1933.
Courtesy Ron Murray

The combination of the seepage under the gates and the flow of the rivers further down, was too great to "dry up" the riverbed. In 1928 a severe winter dropped the Kawarau two feet lower than it had ever been, even with the gates closed, without revealing the "golden harvest". After that the project died a natural death. Once again the mighty Clutha had triumphed and continued to flow uninterrupted down to the sea.

Scotland Point

As if to make amends for the farce of the Kawarau Dam, in 1932 a rich strike of gold was made at Scotland Point at the lower end of the Kawarau Gorge. Prior to this, in 1862 a prospector by the name of Scotland[3] had found some gold at Scotland Point (hence the name). Seventy years later in October 1932, two sets of brothers, the Bells and the Hoopers, and W. Kilgour elected to drive two tunnels into a sandstone bluff at Scotland Point, where "old Scotland" had discovered gold in 1862. They were rewarded by a seam of rich-bearing wash appearing in the roof of both tunnels. Significantly the tunnels were immediately above the spot where the *Lady Ranfurly* dredge had earlier secured its record returns (see Chapter 13).

Almost overnight a forest of claim pegs appeared on the large river flats between Cromwell and the entrance to the Kawarau Gorge. Some of these claims were in the most absurd[2] and unlikely places, even in the surrounding hills, such was the mad scramble for gold. An atmosphere of optimism and enthusiasm existed with could be likened to that of eight years before, when the Kawarau Dam got under way. Tunnels were driven by miners adjacent to the two successful mines, but significantly none of these showed any gold. Notwithstanding, they sold out for large sums of money. After a few weeks of modest returns the Bell-Kilgour and Bell-Hooper mines[2] shrewdly sold out for a handsome 18,000 pounds each and both mines soon petered out. Other claim holders who were bold enough to sink exploratory shafts into their claims on the Cromwell flats had only empty holes to show for their labours. Another Kawarau boom had bust!

Kawarau Gorge Mining Centre

In 1981 the government purchased the old goldmining area at Gee's Flat in the lower Kawarau Gorge. This reserve is now under the control of DOC and is leased as a display centre where the visitor can see all the items of equipment and the techniques used by the old timers in their search for gold. Although a tourist centre, its location in the unspoiled Kawarau Gorge gives it an atmosphere of genuine authenticity. Self-guided and guided tours are available, the latter including working demonstrations of a sluice gun and a quartz crushing battery. It is here that the puzzled layman learns that a "battery" is not an electric battery, as so many people understandably think, but a battery of heavy stamps, or weights, that pound up and down in a box containing quartz, crushing the quartz to release its gold.

Within the reserve a replica of a Chinese camp has been constructed, modelled on the old Chinatown at Cromwell. Genuine early Chinese and European rock shelters can also be seen on a longer loop walk.

The earliest reference to anyone mining at Gee's Flat is in 1864 when Irving[3] and party

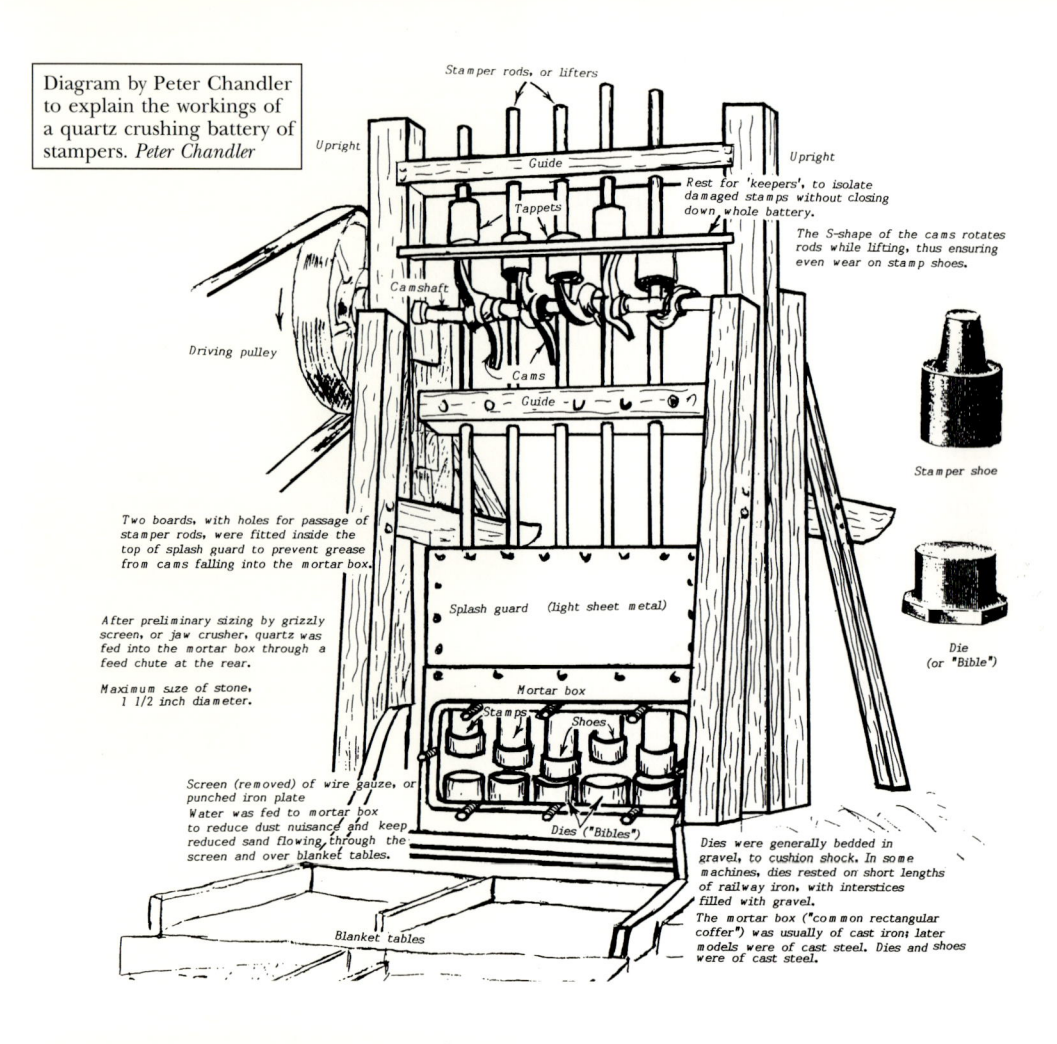

Diagram by Peter Chandler to explain the workings of a quartz crushing battery of stampers. *Peter Chandler*

Stamper rods, or lifters

Upright

Guide

Upright

Tappets

Rest for 'keepers', to isolate damaged stamps without closing down whole battery.

The S-shape of the cams rotates rods while lifting, thus ensuring even wear on stamp shoes.

Camshaft

Driving pulley

Cams

Guide

Stamper shoe

Two boards, with holes for passage of stamper rods, were fitted inside the top of splash guard to prevent grease from cams falling into the mortar box.

After preliminary sizing by grizzly screen, or jaw crusher, quartz was fed into the mortar box through a feed chute at the rear.

Maximum size of stone, 1 1/2 inch diameter.

Splash guard (light sheet metal)

Die (or "Bible")

Mortar box

Stamps   Shoes

Screen (removed) of wire gauze, or punched iron plate

Water was fed to mortar box to reduce dust nuisance and keep reduced sand flowing through the screen and over blanket tables.

Dies ("Bibles")

Dies were generally bedded in gravel, to cushion shock. In some machines, dies rested on short lengths of railway iron, with interstices filled with gravel.

The mortar box ("common rectangular coffer") was usually of cast iron; later models were of cast steel. Dies and shoes were of cast steel.

Blanket tables

Below: Cage for crossing the Kawarau River at the mining centre.

Demonstration quartz crushing battery at Kawarau Gorge Mining Centre.

Rev. Alexander Don, missionary to the Chinese miners, crossing the Clutha River in a chair.
Otago Settlers Museum

The unique line of seven berdans in front of the Invincible battery.

were "tunnelling from the river into Gee's Flat". But who Gee was nobody knows. Gee is both an European and Chinese name and a Chinese miner by the name of Gee is known to have worked in nearby Potters Gully.

HEAD OF LAKE WAKATIPU

Gold was found in the Dart and Rees Rivers at the head of Lake Wakatipu, but it was a pittance compared with the golden rivers of the Queenstown basin, the Shotover and Arrow.

Invincible mine

In 1879 a shepherd, Thomas Hope[2], discovered a gold reef high above the bushline on the mountain wall of the Rees Valley. In 1880 a company was formed with a view to erecting a quartz crushing battery on location at the reef. A steep zig-zag track was constructed up through the bush to convey the heavy machinery up to the site. By November 1882 the ten-stamper battery was ready for an initial crushing, which resulted in 325 ounces of gold. Several tunnels were driven into the mountainside above the battery and the ore was trucked down to a wooden chute which fed the battery. The battery in its weather-boarded battery house was driven by a large water wheel, using water delivered by a water race from Invincible Creek.

Queenstown, Lake Wakatipu, 1868. Painting by J. T. Thomson. *Hall-Jones family.*

For a few years the Invincible mine operated with some success, actually returning small but regular dividends to its shareholders, which was quite a rarity in quartz mining. Then in 1887 things came to a sudden end.

The circular concrete buddle on the valley floor, far below the Invincible mine. *DOC*

The reef was lost! The writing was on the wall and although several attempts were made to relocate the reef, it was never found and in 1897 the mine finally closed down. From the initial crushing in 1882 to the final closure in 1897 the Invincible mine returned 7,500 ounces of gold.

Two special features of the Invincible mine were its line of seven berdans at the battery site and a large concrete buddle, far below on the valley floor. The unique line of berdans, mounted on a wooden frame, is still in place in front of the battery making the steep climb up to the mine well worthwhile. (These berdans, or cast iron bowls, slowly rotated with heavy weights inside to further pulverise the crushed quartz.)

The equally unique buddle, or concentrator, is also still in place alongside the Rees Valley Road. Tailings from the

The Invincible battery, high on the mountainside of Rees Valley. *Burton Bros*

The Dart River dredge. Dredgemaster Hay standing in front. Behind him, Mark Harris, the dredge cook.
Lakes District Museum

battery were shot down a 680 metre wooden chute to the circular dome-shaped buddle made of concrete. The sorted tailings were placed on the stationary surface of the buddle and jets of water from four rotating arms were played on the ore to separate out the lighter sand from the heavier gold, which fell into gutters on the perimeter.

Dart River dredge

In 1899 a company was formed with the aim of placing a gold dredge on the Dart River. The dredge, including the pontoons, would be built of local timber, the machinery manufactured in Dunedin. By March 1900[5] all the construction work had been completed and the dredge was ready for launching at Dredge Flat on the Dart River.

But from the very beginning everything seemed to go wrong. The bucket ladder was too short to allow dredging at any depth. The hull was too light to resist bucking whenever the dredge struck a boulder. The tailings chute was useless because it had a right-angled bend in it where the tailings got stuck. To cap this off, the whole dredge was too small to handle the sudden, frequent floods in the Dart River, which meant that there were many days when it couldn't work and on at least nine occasions it was left high and dry after the floods receded.[5]

Although dredgemaster Hay did his best to cope with the multiple failings of the dredge he had been given, with poor returns of gold, the company had no option but to go into liquidation in 1901. In 1903 the dredge was dismantled, the machinery sold off and the woodwork left on Dredge Flat, where the rotting remains of the pontoons and tailings elevator lie in a hollow.

REFERENCES
1. Gilkison, Robert, *Early Days in Central Otago*, 1930
2. Sinclair, R. S. M., *Kawarau Gold*, 1962
3. Parcell, J. C., *Heart of the Desert*, 1951
4. Chandler, Peter, *Head of Lake Wakatipu*, 1984
5. Paulin, Pat, *Dart River Gold Dredge*, 2003

CHAPTER 12
The Maniototo Goldfields

*By and by a few black dots appeared
and then wreaths of smoke began to ascend.
The miners had come out of their tents.*
J. G. Bremner, 1863

As the hordes of eager prospectors streamed across the Maniototo section of the Dunstan Road to the Dunstan diggings, a party of Cornishmen stopped at Moa Ceek (near Poolburn), where they discovered gold in March 1863.[5] The Cornishmen opted to stay put and mine at Moa Creek instead of continuing on to Dunstan. They established a little community of stone huts in the wide open valley of Moa Creek, which was so named because of the large number of moa skeletons that were found in the valley's swamp.

The Cornish miners continued mining at Moa Creek for seventeen years until 1870, when Chinese miners took over and worked there for another 40 years until 1910, when dredges moved into the valley.

Keith Falconer, the owner of the Moa Creek diggings, has restored a number of the Cornish and Chinese stone huts and has opened the valley for tours.

Among the Cornish and Chinese stone huts is an old chimney relic with an unique herring-bone pattern at its base, which Dr James Ng[12] informed me is not of Chinese origin, but a typical Cornish pattern. On the other hand, the stone huts with rounded chimneys and doorways beside the chimney at one end of the hut, are typically Chinese. This is in contrast to the European huts, where the doorway is typically placed in the middle of the front wall.

On 21 June 2004, at a moving ceremony during the Otago Goldfields Heritage Trust's visit to Moa Creek, Dr Ng and Duncan Sew Hoy, a direct descendant of the famous Choie Sew Hoy, unveiled a plaque to the Chinese

Chimney relic at Moa Creek with unique herring-bone pattern, which is typically Cornish.

Typical Chinese stone hut at Moa Creek, with rounded chimney beside doorway at one end of the hut.

Goldfields of Otago

Dr James Ng and Duncan Sew Hoy unveiling a plaque in 2004 to the early Cornish and Chinese miners at Moa Creek.

and Cantonese prospectors who mined for gold at Moa Creek from 1863 to 1910.

Naseby

In May 1863, two months after gold was discovered at Moa Creek, the Parker brothers,[1] William and Richard, trekked up the Manuherikia Valley from Alexandra and across the Maniototo Plain to Coal Pit Gully, on the southwest side of the future town of Naseby. There, where a roadside plaque now marks the spot, they first found gold. Then following up the Hogburn Gully to its head they found better payable gold, a few hundred metres above the future town. For a month they worked away quietly, but the word got out and the Naseby rush was on.[2] By July, five gullies were being mined in the Hogburn, with the Parkers in the middle. By 26 July a 'canvas town' of about '2,000' people had been set up in Lollywoman's Gully with a main 'street' of 18 stores, two butchers' shops and a bakery.

But this 'tent town' was too close to the sluicings and soon shifted down to the mouth of Hogburn Gully, where a new town, Hogburn, was laid out. The name Hogburn was retained for a number of years, then in 1869 it was changed to Naseby, the birthplace of John Hyde Harris, the Superintendent of Otago.

Naseby was an unusual goldfield in that it was so close to the sluicings, that most of the miners walked back to the town for the night. Only one or two hardy types dwelt among the sluicings, a cold and miserable place in the winter. Early mining in the gully was by the simple

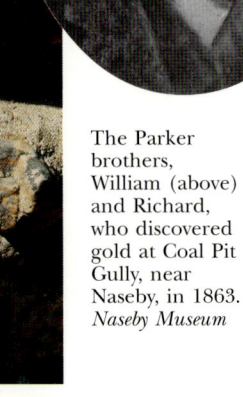

The Parker brothers, William (above) and Richard, who discovered gold at Coal Pit Gully, near Naseby, in 1863. *Naseby Museum*

Plaque at Coal Pit Road, Naseby, commemorating the Parker brothers' discovery of gold in 1863.

method of sluice boxes. Thus Naseby acquired the reputation of being a 'poorman's field'. Not because the returns were low, but because very little capital was required to set up a claim. Mining continued steadily in the Hogburn for many years, except for a 'hiccup' in the 1870s when the tailings channel became silted up. By 1872 Naseby township was threatened by piles of tailings along its main street, up to six metres high! The solution was a major water race, the Mt Ida race, and a sludge channel, which were eventually opened in 1877.

The Maniototo Rush

With the discoveries of gold by the Cornishmen at Moa Creek and the Parker Brothers at Hogburn (Naseby) miners rushed into the Manuherikia Valley and the Maniototo, prospecting the mountainous flanks to trigger off a whole series of new discoveries, with the eruption of a multitude of associated gold towns. Miners approaching the Maniototo by the Taieri Valley from Dunedin discovered gold at Hyde, Hamiltons and Serpentine at the head of the Taieri River.

Mt Ida water race, which is still used today for irrigation.

Early Naseby, with sludge channel from Hogburn Gully on right. *Otago Settlers Museum*

Chinese miners sluicing in Spec Gully, Naseby, 1901.
Alexander Turnbull Library

Left: Old sluicings at Hogburn Gully today.

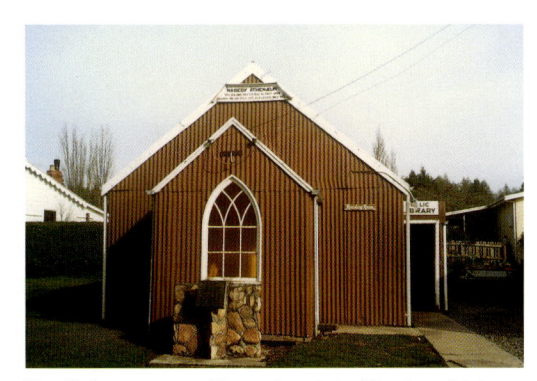

The little corrugated iron church in Naseby, which later became the Athenaeum and now the library.

By August 1863 there were 5,000[1] miners working in the new goldfield and 4,320 ounces of gold had been brought out by the first gold escort to Dunedin.

The gold towns

One of the best accounts of the gold towns that sprang up with the various rushes in the new goldfield comes from the narrative of John Gault Bremner,[3] who with his two brothers, Joseph and Robert, established a store in Naseby in 1863, with branches in the other gold towns.

John Bremner arrived in the original 'tent town' in the Hogburn in August 1863. The few stores on the diggings were just "calico buildings 12 x 16 feet" and the population at the gold rush was "some 400-500 people".

> "I will not soon forget the dreary sight that met me the morning after my arrival. Looking up the gully, everything was white, a rather heavy fall of snow having taken place the night previous. Now the hard frost, which usually follows, held everything in its grasp. By and by, a few black moving dots appeared and then wreaths of smoke began to ascend. The miners had come out of their 6 x 8 tents – rigged mostly by ropes run from two upright sticks, or even long handled shovels, the ends of the ropes being tied to tussock grass.
>
> It was a most depressing sight, no firewood, all bleak and barren, wet and cold, and any coal procurable was wet. Matagouri was very little better, so the poor fellows had to fall back on grass, feeding the fire with handfuls of it. To boil the billy and cook a chop was no easy matter. Under these conditions, you can imagine how eagerly and thankfully the miners would receive any case wood the storekeepers would give them. The givers were not forgotten by the recipients, as I had good reason to know in after and better days.
>
> However, as we were now in September and Spring was on us, things improved, but I think that winter was the severest that had been experienced. It may be that people were not so well provided with means to withstand the inclemency of the weather."

John's brother, Joseph, had preceded him and had erected their store on the site of the future Royal Hotel in Naseby. Soon there were 21 public houses and business places of every kind and the new town became a busy little spot."

Today one of the oldest and quaintest buildings in Naseby is the little corrugated iron hut, now used as a library. Originally built as the first church in Naseby it became the Athenaeum in 1873, where Professor James Black of Otago University gave a series of well-attended lectures on the geology and assaying of gold.

Mt Burster (Buster)

Soon after Bremner's arrival the Mt Burster (widely known as Mt Buster or just plain 'Buster') opened up and a big rush set in up the hill.

> "Great expectations were held that an extensive field would be opened up on this big watershed of the Waitaki. These were doomed to disappointment, only a small patch of auriferous ground being found. It soon became a field occupied by a a few parties who however, did very well for some years. A small town sprang up at the foot of the Buster and I put up a nice little iron store, 18 x 20 feet."[3]

Hamiltons

In October 1863 Brockleman's party discovered gold on Captain James Hamilton's run on the northern slopes of the Rock and Pillar Range.[4] The discovery was not reported in the press until 12 December and was at first thought to be a hoax. When the truth was realised, virtually the whole of Naseby 'decamped' (by then a population of 2,000) to the new rush in a matter of days. Foremost amongst the Naseby people was John Bremner, always on the lookout for business.[3]

> "When the new rush was reported at Hamiltons, I locked up my Buster store and rode to Naseby and thence to Hamiltons. Got a good site from Black Pat – that is the only name I had for him. He saw me ride up and sang out, 'Here you are. I was looking for you and kept my tent here till you would come.' He would not take anything for the site. I think I forced 5 pounds on him, but I was

Sluicings and holding dam at Hamiltons, one of the richest goldfields in the Maniototo.

Small bucket and ladder dredge which worked from a barge in the Taieri River near Sowburn (Patearoa).

of the smaller Maniototo goldfields and for a time it eclipsed the Naseby field.[4] Within 18 months, 80,000 ounces of gold were recovered from the shallow ground. Good returns continued until 1868, then the special gold escort laid on for Hamiltons was discontinued and reverted to the Naseby escort.

Today Hamiltons is but a ghost town, only a rock-walled cemetery, the sluicings and holding dam remain.

Close to Hamiltons a small rush took place at Sowburn[3] (Patearoa), while the Hamiltons rush was in full swing. Although this rush was short-lived and attracted only 200-300 miners, there are some interesting relics at Sowburn today, including miners' huts and a sluicing monitor. Also a gold dredge, mounted alongside the road south of Patearoa.

told afterwards that he had refused 10 pounds for the ground. I think he must have got some case wood in the early days and had not forgot. I posted up a notice, 'Bremner Bros'. This would hold the ground for 48 hours."

Riding overnight Bremner returned to his "Buster" store, packed up all the goods on the shelves and made for Hamiltons in time to save his site from being "jumped".

Hamiltons proved to be easily the richest

Hyde

Gold was discovered at Hyde shortly after the Hamiltons rush began, by some miners on their way up the Taieri River to Hamiltons The Hyde diggings were on the north side of the township of Hyde, which was named after

The Hyde diggings and original town of Hyde (north of the present one). Mine shafting in foreground. *Otago Settlers Museum*

Superintendent John Hyde Harris. "Hyde's shallow-ground gold was quickly worked out", Bremner informs us,[3] "and the pan and cradle miners then left the field to a few sluicing parties".

Drybread and Tinkers

The Manuherikia Valley goldfields extended into the gullies of the Dunstan Mts, where gold bearing streams were found at Drybread and Tinkers (two delightful names). One popular version of the origin of the name, Drybread, is that two early miners had a goat which they used to milk when they wanted to sop their dry bread. The origin of the name, Tinkers, is similarly debatable. June Wood[5] suggests that the name was derived from the miners' cagey answer to the query, "How are doing"? To which the reply was, "Just tinkering". But it could be equally said that the miners' tents looked like a 'Tinkers camp'. The name Tinkers survived until 1887, when it was officially changed to Matakanui, another example of George Griffiths' *Spurious Maori Place-Names*.[6]

Thanks to the Scottish artist Andrew Hamilton we have a sketch of Drybread c.1869 (see illustration overleaf). But apart from the remains of the diggings and the Drybread cemetery, there is little to be seen today.

At Tinkers, on the other hand, there is a lot to see. With the major sluicings that went on at Tinkers, both the Drybread school and an hotel shifted down to Tinkers. The old Drybread school, with its bell-tower, survives as a woolshed in a farm paddock and the hotel was renamed Newtown Tavern,

Mounted sluice gun (monitor) at Tinkers, 1979.

Andrew Hamilton's sketch of Drybread c.1869. *Hamilton's sketchbook.*

Sluicing the Undaunted claim at Tinkers (Matakanui). *Hocken Library*

The Maniototo Goldfields 151

Andrew Hamilton's sketch of Cambrians in 1869. Hamilton's sketchbook

The old Drybread School which was shifted down to Tinkers and is now used as a woolshed. Note school bell-tower.

The ex-Drybread Hotel which became the Newtown Tavern, Matakanui.

The Tinkers store and post office which was previously used as the office of the Mt Morgan Sluicing Co. Note mudbrick walls.

Matakanui. Also surviving is the old general store and post office, which was once the registered office of the "Mt Morgan Sluicing Co. Ltd". Also in the village, there is an impressive sluice gun (monitor), which once operated in the sluicings to the west of the town.

Tinkers is on the road to Thomsons Gorge through the Dunstan Mts, which links it with the rich Bendigo field on the far side.

Cambrians

Thanks again to Andrew Hamilton we have a sketch of Welshmans Gully, where a party

Cambrians goldfield in the 1880s. Note walled paddocks. *Burton Bros*

Left: Surviving mudbrick wall of the Welsh Harp Hotel, Cambrians.

of Welsh miners worked and lived in their settlement at Cambrians, an alternative name for Welshmen. In 1864 Owen J. Owen erected a calico chapel at Cambrians, where prayer meetings were conducted in Welsh.[5]

As you take the side road to Cambrians, notice the lonely, unknown grave on the corner, with its weathered wooden enclosure, the mound carefully sluiced around by the miners and left in peace. Cambrians has survived as a delightful little holiday resort of carefully kept cottages. On the left as you enter the township, notice the crumbling mudbrick wall of what was once the Welsh Harp Hotel. In Welshmans Gully there are some impressive remains of sluicings.

St Bathans

In November 1863 a prospecting party, which included the Irish photographer Peyman, discovered gold in Dunstan Creek at the foot of Mt St Bathans (named by J. T. Thomson after his mother's home). They were not left to enjoy their harvest for long, for within four months there were 200-300 miners on the ground and a substantial 'tent city' on the site of the future St Bathans. But it was not an orderly 'city' and the *Cromwell Argus* reports it as:[7]

"The buildings and their appurtenances are constructed of all kinds of material, amongst which

The Maniototo Goldfields

Lonely grave and sluicings on the road to Cambrians. Dunstan Mountains behind.

I may mention corrugated iron, red iron, tin, gin cases, staves, and canvas. The street is the narrowest I have ever seen – unless, indeed, those of Constantinople; and in the very centre of the township there stands conspicuously a huge pig-stye, generally full of fat pigs, and surrounded with the heads and horns of animals. The effluvium rising out of the locality on a warm day is enough to create a malarious fever; it is positively sickening. Passing hurriedly by, the stranger carefully guides his horses through the labyrinth of children, broken bones, carpenters tools, bottles, salmon-tins and miscellaneous rubbish until he emerges into an esplanade a degree more healthy than the street behind him."

The jumble of buildings in early St Bathans is illustrated in the sketch by Andrew

Andrew Hamilton's sketch of the "jumble" of buildings in St Bathans c.1869. Hamilton's sketchbook.

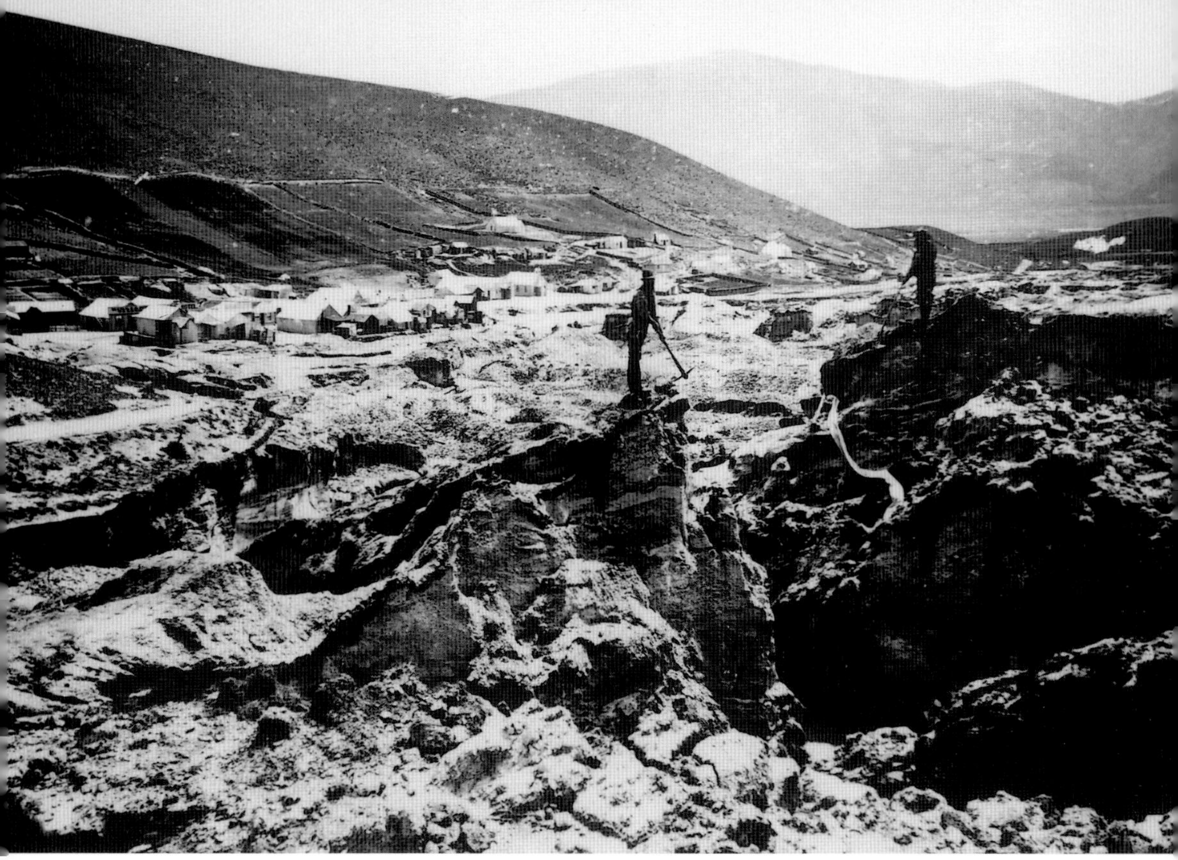

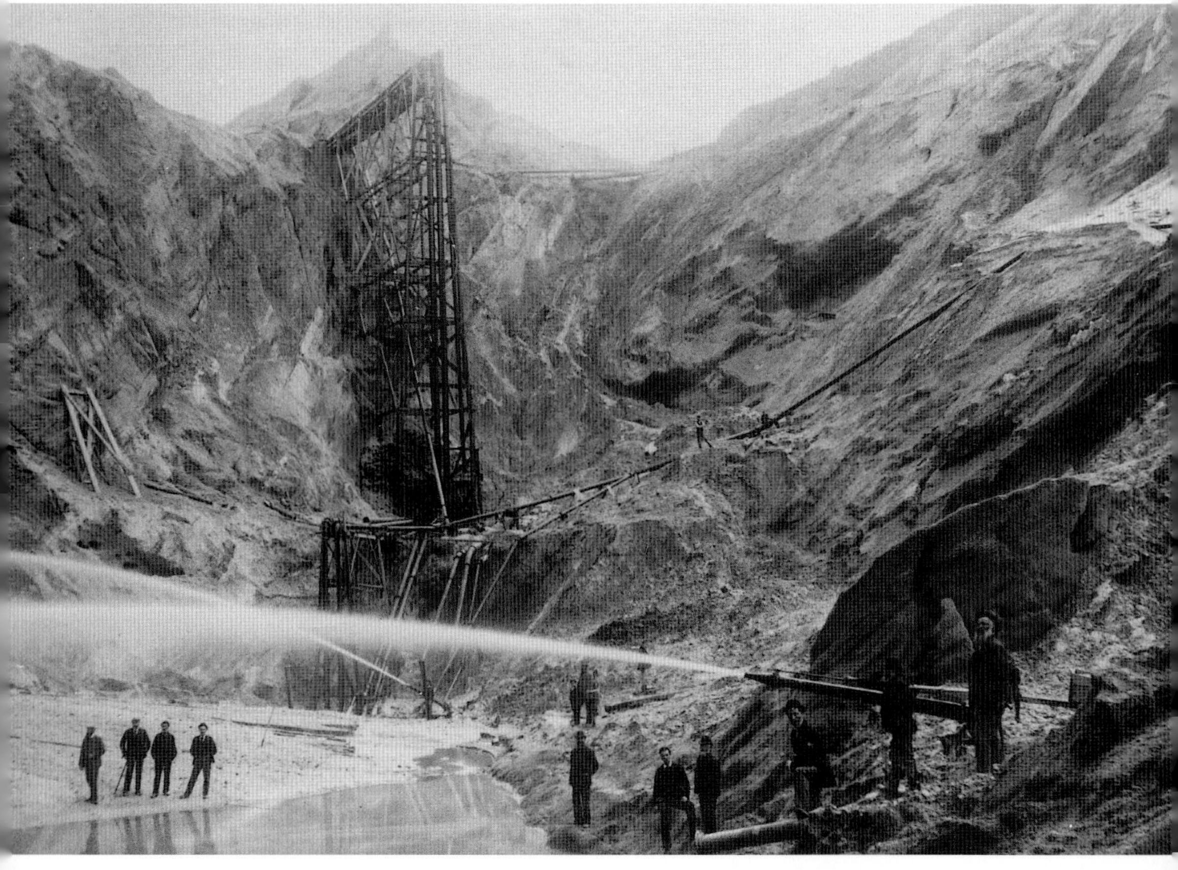

Hamilton. Wooden buildings soon replaced the canvas and corrugated iron huts and within a year there were ten hotels and many other places of business lining the single narrow street. The little community also supported two churches and two schools. Rather than a 'boom' town St Bathans was now a service centre for a relatively stable mining population of 500-700. The main centre of mining operations was on Kildare Hill, opposite the town on a spur of Mt St Bathans. Named in honour of a party of Irishmen from Kildare who mined it, the hill was originally 120 metres high and stood where the Blue Lake now lies. The miners progressively sluiced away Kildare Hill and by 1870 "every particle of it had been demolished and sent seaward".[8]

In the early 1880s the innovative John Ewing installed hydraulic elevators on the Kildare claim, which he proceeded to work to greater and greater depths with no sign of the gold bottoming out. In the early 1900s the Scandanavian Company took over Ewing's claim and by 1907 it was elevating on a scale unheard of in New Zealand.[8] It continued to win gold till the 1920s, when the depth of the gold dirt became too great to elevate. Hydraulic elevating was started again in 1933 with the greatest lift in the world,[8] 68.8 metres, in two stages. But this was stopped in 1934 because of the risk to St Bathans township. The 'glory hole' of the Kildare claim began to fill with water, leaving the deepest workings submerged under the waters of Blue Lake.

Today St Bathans is a charming, peaceful little town of beautifully maintained historic buildings[9] blending in perfectly with tall mature trees. Here are the old Vulcan Hotel and wooden billiards saloon, the stone school and school house, two churches, the public hall and private cottages. The grandly designed two-storeyed wooden post office was built more recently in 1909.

Facing page, above: Miners demolishing Kildare Hill at St Bathans, 1879. St Bathans township on left. *Lakes District Museum*

Facing page, below: Elevator and sluice gun working in the 'great hole' that was once Kildare Hill, 1899. *Alexandra Museum*

Below: The resultant Blue Lake at St Bathans.

"Gone are the dancing girls, the numerous hotels, the banks, the hundreds of diggers – and all those things that follow the discovery of gold – they are gone from St Bathans. But St Bathans is not gone.

No! It is a town – a very small town – blessed with glorious sunny days, star-lit nights and rich in hospitality and friendship. And the Blue Lake of St Bathans – that remains as a monument to the gold miners of early history and is a gem of indescribably beauty. These things are St Bathans today."[10]

The old Vulcan Hotel and billiards saloon at St Bathans.

Restored bank and gold office at St Bathans.

Blacks (Ophir)

Blacks was named after the owners of the original homestead, which preceded the goldfield days.[5] Later it became known as Blacks No. 1 to distinguish it from the nearby German Hill diggings, which were known as Blacks Nos 2 and 3. Then it became Ophir, which is its name today.

In 1866 Blacks was reported as the "best poorman's diggings on the goldfield, where no newcomer could miss getting gold if he sank a shaft to 5 feet on the terraces or flats towards the river [Manuherikia]".[5]

The town supported a stable mining population for many years and Cobb & Co always changed horses here before the coach went on to Tinkers.

Today many of the old buildings in Ophir have been restored, making a stroll down the tranquil main street a most rewarding experience. Here amongst many historic buildings, are the Bungalow, the retirement home of the Rev. Alexander Don and his wife, the old gaol and the charming little post office, built in 1886 and now an Historic

Restored hut of the miner Lochart MacTavish, outside Ophir.

"The Bungalow", the retirement cottage of the Rev. Alexander Don and his wife.

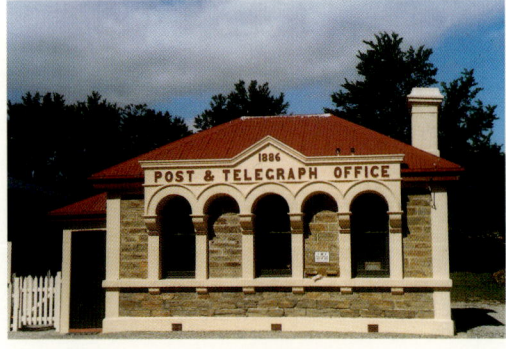

Post Office built at Ophir in 1886.

Andrew Hamilton's sketch of Blacks No. 1 (Ophir), 1869. *Hamilton's sketchbook. Below:* Sluiced face and tailings at German Hill, 2004.

Places Trust building. As you enter the town from Poolburn Road you pass the restored hut of the miner MacTavish and as you leave the town you cross the historic Daniel O'Connell bridge.

German Hill

Gold was first discovered at German Hill, on the lower slopes of Rough Ridge, by Henry Carr's party[11] in November 1864. Being one of the last rushes in the Maniototo goldfield it gathered in miners from all round the district.[3]

The Bremner Bros established a store there and, interestingly, John Bremner records[3] that one of the other stores was owned by Philip Levy, one of the infamous Maungatua gang of robbers who was probably using it to obtain information. Bremner informs us that "the town had a top street running along the foot of German Hill and a long street of business places, fully a quarter of a mile long, straight out from the workings into the flat below".

"The auriferous deposit was in some places fairly rich in gold, but the ground was limited", writes Bremner. This was because of the lack of fall for the sluicings channel[11]. Within six months the 850 miners who had descended on the German Hill diggings had exhausted the field and with the state of the West Coast gold rush they moved speedily away, leaving a large sluiced basin on German Hill.

In his archaeological assessment of the German Hill field in 1993, Peter Bristow[11] records that Frederick Rowley was running the Aultbea Hotel at German Hill in 1875 and that John Beattie had the hotel from 1878-79. In 1879 Beattie put the hotel on sale, which included a stable, stockyard, garden and paddocks. The substantial remains of the Aultbea Hotel (the name comes from Wester Ross, Scotland) are still there, also those of another hotel.

Garibaldi diggings

On the opposite side of Rough Ridge from German Hill were the Garibaldi diggings, which were worked by a party of Italians, hence the name. Situated near the Murison brothers pioneer Puketoi station, the little settlement is remarkable for its alignment of the Italian miners' huts, a veritable "miners' row".

Serpentine

The rush to the Serpentine began in June 1863,[13] when prospectors found gold in the Serpentine Valley at the head of the Taieri River.

Following up a branch of Serpentine Creek to a flat basin (Golden Gully) below the summit of Rough Ridge, they established the township of Serpentine. At an elevation of over 1,000 metres it was the highest gold town in Otago and possibly New Zealand. There were three stores and hotels, a cottage school and a cemetery in the township and in 1873 a stone church was built.

According to local legend the minister arrived late for the opening of the church in 1873, only to find the congregation had been whiling away the time drinking in the pub. After the first hymn the congregation demanded an encore with great enthusiasm and got an extra sermon for their pains! Few ministers subsequently bothered to make the arduous journey to Serpentine again and by 1902 (and probably earlier) the church was being lived in by three miners. Later it was used as a shelter by musterers and rabbiters. Today the lonely stone church is the sole surviving building at Serpentine and stands

Remains of the Aultbea Hotel, German Hill, 2004.

"Miner's row" at Garibaldi diggings, Gimmerburn.

Serpentine Church, 1979.

Above, right: Sod hut at Golden Gully, Serpentine, 1931.
Otago Settlers Museum

Serpentine battery and water wheel in Long Gully.

in solitude in this remote, desolate place.

Mining, including sluicing and tunnelling, took place in the Golden Gully and when a quartz reef was discovered in 1878 a battery was set up at German Jacks.

One of the Golden Gully mines was on the summit of Rough Ridge. In 1890 the Serpentine battery was taken over the summit and down into the Long Valley beyond, to service the mine 300 metres above. The ore from the mine was lowered on a steep tramline for crushing at the ten stamper battery, which was driven by a "26 foot wide water wheel".[14]

The mine was not a success and the battery ceased operations in 1891. Nevertheless the ten stamper battery and its water wheel remain together, the only surviving pair in Otago.[14] Likewise the ruins of the miner's stone huts are still on the summit ridge above.

Oturehua

The Golden Progress quartz mine at Oturehua is notable for its intact poppet head, the only surviving one in the Otago goldfields. Most poppet heads were built of wood and eventually rotted away. But the Golden Progress poppet head was constructed of Australian hardwood and erected later than most, in 1928, which explains its survival.

The mine was worked by three lignite-fired boilers (with strikingly tall chimneys) two for the poppet head to drive the winding gear and the other to drive the battery further down the gully.

One of the boilers of the Golden Progress mine.

Surviving poppet head of the Golden Progress mine at Oturehua.

The upper Kyeburn diggings on the road to Dansey Pass. Edwin George's Dansey Pass Hotel and butchery in foreground. *Hocken Library*

Dansey Pass Hotel in the 1920s. Note sign, "Tea at all hours". *Hocken Library*

Chinese miners sluicing in the upper Kyeburn, 1901. *Hocken Library*

In 1937 the mine was closed down and the battery removed to Bendigo.[13]

Kyeburn Diggings, Dansey Pass

According to John Bremner,[3] Edwin George built his original Dansey Pass Hotel and butchery in 1860, which was before gold mining began at Dansey Pass. Edwin George was not a gold miner, but he built his hotel in the upper Kyeburn Valley because it was on a direct route to the Maerewhenua diggings across Dansey Pass.

In 1861 Leggatt[15] discovered rich gold, "not much waterworn" and "half-pea nuggety" in the upper Kyeburn Valley. The new field would "pay three ounces a day", the discoverer claimed.

With the rush that followed, George rebuilt his hotel in stone and expanded his butchery business to include a store and bakery.

The stonemason who built the hotel was known only as "Happy Bill" and, according to local legend, he took his payment in beer.

Recently the Dansey Pass Hotel has been completely renovated and is now a popular stopping place for travellers crossing the pass. The stone ruins opposite the front of the hotel are the remains of the hotel stables, which were later used as a garage.

Sergeant Garvey

In September 1863 Sergeant Edward Garvey of the mounted constabulary perished in a snowstorm at the foot of Mt Kyeburn the circumstances were these:

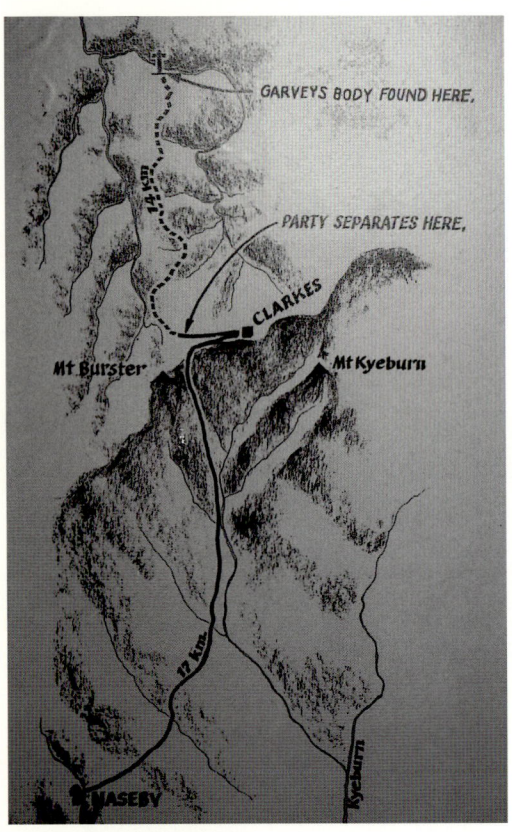

Sketch map of Sergeant Garvey's route from Naseby in 1863. *Naseby Museum*

Police historian speaking at the dedication of the cairn where Sergeant Garvey's body was found. The Commissioner of Police standing behind. *R. Harraway*

23 Sept. Sergeant Garvey and trooper McDonald were sent from Naseby to report on the new goldfield at Clarkes Gully (between Mts Kyeburn and Burster). They arrive at Clarkes where they spend the night.

24 Sept. Garvey and McDonald, accompanied by Magee, a baker, set out for Naseby, but they are caught in a snowstorm and, becoming disorientated, they disagree about the direction they should take. Garvey, mistakenly, continues north (instead of south to Naseby), while the other two sleep out in the open.

25 Sept. McDonald and Magee awake to find that they are only one mile from Clarkes, which they return to before starting out for Naseby. They leave Clarkes at midday, but spend another night out in the open.

26 Sept. McDonald (by now frostbitten) and Magee arrive exhausted in Naseby to find that Garvey has not turned up. Sergeant

Ryan sends out two troopers and a guide to search for Garvey.
- 27 Sept. The search party returns to Naseby having found no sign of Garvey.
- 28 Sept. Detective Rowley and a party of volunteers set out to search for Garvey.
- 30 Sept. North of Clarkes the searchers pick up the hoof prints of Garvey's horse which they follow for 14 kilometres until they come across the horse, grazing, with Garvey's body lying under a large rock nearby (a stone cairn was erected there). The body is brought back to Naseby.
- 5 Oct. At the inquest in Dunedin it was found that Garvey had died of exposure. He was aged only 30 at the time of his death.

Popular amongst the miners, Garvey had served in the Crimean War where he was awarded the French Legion of Honour. (Recently the stone cairn was rebuilt and was dedicated to Garvey at a ceremony attended by the Commissioner of Police.)

Macraes

In May 1862 gold was discovered in Deepdell Creek by James Crombie[16] and his mates. As miners flocked to the new field more discoveries were made in the surrounding creeks and the township of Macraes sprang up on Macraes Flat, three kilometres south of Deepdell. At first it was a 'canvas town' and then a number of fine stone buildings appeared, including the popular Stanley's Hotel which is still in use today. There was also quite a large Chinese camp at the town with two stores owned by Ah Nam. One of the Chinese mud-brick cottages at Macraes, Gay Tan's, is in the process of being restored. Likewise, a number of old stone buildings and walls at Macraes have been carefully preserved, making a visit to the gold town well worthwhile. Recently the Macraes Mining Co. has developed an excellent interpretation centre in the town.

The main focus of the gold mining at Macraes was at Golden Point, Deepdell Creek, three kilometres north of the town. At first it was potholing. Then in 1890 the Donaldson brothers opened up a quartz reef and began crushing for both gold and scheelite (the ore of tungsten). The Donaldsons' battery

Stanley's motto.

Stanley's Hotel at Macraes. *Otago Settlers Museum*

had a long and successful life (1890-1953) and in a twenty year period of operations it produced 10,000 ounces of gold and 500 tons of scheelite. The Donaldsons exported their first bags of scheelite to Great Britain in 1892 and during both World Wars, when tungsten prices soared, the Macraes' miners enjoyed buoyant times. Although the Donaldsons' battery was broken up for scrap in 1953 its foundations remain behind Jim Callery's house, opposite the Callerys' battery.

The existing five stamper battery at Golden

Gay Tan's mudbrick cottage at Macraes Flat.

The "village pump" outside the bakery at Macraes. The baker, T. Powis, on right.
Otago Settlers Museum

The Callery brothers' battery and shed at Golden Point.

Jim Callery's house at Golden Point. The foundations of the earlier Donaldsons' battery lie beneath the macrocarpa tree on right.

Oceana Gold's processing plant on Golden Point Road.

Point (the Callery brothers') was originally built in 1902. Then in the late 1920s, the Callery brothers, Jim, Phil and Ned, took over, mining on Round Hill on the south side of Deepdell. Later Hughie Fraser managed the battery, which continued to operate right into the 1950s.

The remarkable feature about the Golden Point battery is that it is the only workable battery on location in the South Island complete with its shed.[13] The battery is protected in the Golden Point reserve, which

Hughie Fraser's mudbrick hut at Golden Point.

Nenthorn, 1889, the only known photograph of the township. *Otago Settlers Museum*

The tiered foundations of the Consolidated battery in Deighton Creek Gorge.

includes the Callery brothers three huts and Hughie Fraser's hut.

In 1989 the Macraes Mining Co (now Oceana Gold) began their gigantic operation of open-cast mining at Round Hill. In its first ten years of production (1989-1999) it produced over one million ounces of gold, at an ever continuing rate, reaching a record annual return in 2004 of 185,175 ounces of gold. As Jim Hamel[13] points out, this makes it Otago's most productive mine ever. The distinctive landscape features produced by this modern open-cast mining, waste stacks and effluent ponds, stand in stark contrast to the small scale mining alongside at the historic Golden Point reserve.

Nenthorn

For quite a time before gold was 'officially' discovered at Nenthorn the McRae girls and the Sutton boys had been washing up gold in Nenthorn Creek using cake tins as gold pans. Then in 1888 the quiet pastoral life in their sleepy little hollow was rudely interrupted when a rabbiter, William McMillan, staked off a claim and rode into Naseby to register it. The news quickly leaked out and as he returned overnight he was 'shadowed' by other horsemen, who had no trouble in at great cost "in a most inaccessible place"[17] on the far side of the Deighton Creek Gorge, it crushed only 600 tons of ore at a loss, before it was closed down in 1890. The short-lived gold rush was over.

Today at Nenthorn there are the remains of Patrick Talty's St Bathans Hotel at one end of the 'street' and a tall stone chimney at the other end. Over in the steep gorge of Deighton Creek are the spectacular tiered foundations and one of the massive twin towers of the Consolidated battery.

Tall stone chimney at Nenthorn, 1979.

Remains of Patrick Talty's hotel, Nenthorn, 2004.

keeping his white horse in view. The rush was on.

By 1889 the township of Nenthorn[17] had been surveyed, with several streets laid out. In actual practice there was just a main street, Gordon Street, with the usual array of hotels, stores, banks, a dance hall, a post office and even a newspaper office for the *Nenthorn Recorder*. The rest of the community scattered themselves among the gullies, rocks and tussocks.[16]

The richest reef was the Croesus, immediately below the township. The Croesus mine produced the largest cake of retorted gold at Nenthorn, one of over 200 ounces. Most of the returns from the other mines were disappointing and they were soon abandoned. Of the several crushing batteries connected with various mines, the largest was the Consolidated ten stamper battery. Built

Like so many other gold mines in the Maniototo goldfield, sheep now graze the lonely hills where miners once worked. At the historic town of Naseby, once the busy centre of the goldfield, tall conifers now cover the sluicings of Hogburn Gully.

REFERENCES
1. Hamel, Jill, *Gold Mines and their Landscapes at Naseby*, 1985.
2. Cowan, Janet, *Down the Years in the Manitoto*, 1947.
3. Bremner, J. G., *Mt Ida Goldfields: a Merchant's Memories*, Edited by J. Rutherford, 1988.
4. Paterson, Audrey, *Hamiltons*, 1980
5. Wood, June, *Gold Trails of Otago*, 1970.
6. Griffiths, George, *Spurious Maori Place-Names*, 2002.
7. *Cromwell Argus*, 1870
8. *St Bathans*, Otago Goldfields Park brochure.
9. Nicholson-Garrett, Gladys, *St Bathans*, 1977.
10. *Central Otago News*, 1948.
11. Bristow, Peter, *An Archaeological Assessment of German Hill*, 1993.
12. Ng, Dr James, *personal communication.*
13. Hamel, Jill, *The Archaeology of Otago*, 2001.
14. Petchey, Peter, *The Serpentine water wheel and battery, Archaeology in New Zealand*, 1996.
15. Pyke, Vincent, *Early Gold Discoveries in Otago*, 1887.
16. Thompson, H. M. *East of the Rock and Pillar*, 1948.
17. Hearn, Terry, *Nenthorn*, 1988.

CHAPTER 13
The New Zealand Dredge

*The miners came to regard the rivers as giant sluice boxes,
in which gold had been collecting in the crevices
since the days of yore.*
Dunstan Times, adapted

As the miners nibbled away at the edges of the mighty Clutha River with their gold pans and cradles, they came to regard the river as a 'giant sluice box', in which gold had been collecting in the crevices since the days of yore. If only they could get at the deep swirling pools there must surely be fabulous fortunes to be made!

From as early as 1862[1] the *Dunstan Times* was promoting the dredging of the Clutha. "The bottom of the Molyneux [Clutha], without doubt, contains untold wealth", it claimed. Later it insisted that at the bottom of the river, gold existed "in almost fabulous quantities". And so evolved what became known as the "New Zealand dredge".

At first it was a very primitive affair. A giant spoon at the end of a dipping arm. The spoon consisted of an iron hoop to which was attached a cowhide or canvas bag to scoop up the gravel, which was then tipped into a sluice box to separate the gravel from the gold content (if any!). Mounted on a punt, these primitive spoon dredges could only work close into the bank and in shallow, still water.

The slow, inefficient spoon dredge was soon ousted by the bucket and ladder dredge. An 'endless' chain of buckets was mounted on a ladder, which dipped into the river and scooped up the gold-bearing gravel, or "wash" as it was called. This bucket and ladder system was driven by the water power of the river itself. The punt was anchored securely to the banks of the river, then using the current of the river, twin water wheels on the sides supplied the power to drive the bucket chain. As such they became known as current wheelers. But as Sinclair[2] points out:

Even this mechanical improvement failed to solve completely the problem of reaching the entire bed of the river. The spoon dredge could not be used except in the quiet waters, and the current wheel dredge could not operate except in the flow of the river, which provided the power to drive the bucket line. Hence the spoon dredge was useless in the current, and the current wheel dredge ineffective in the shallows and backwaters. Both, however, sufficed to prove that a machine which could operate independently of the current was likely to

Dunedin merchant Choie Sew Hoy and his son Kum Poy. *Lyndel Soper*

Choie Sew Hoy's dredge, which worked successfully at Big Beach on the Lower Shotover River in 1889. *National Museum*

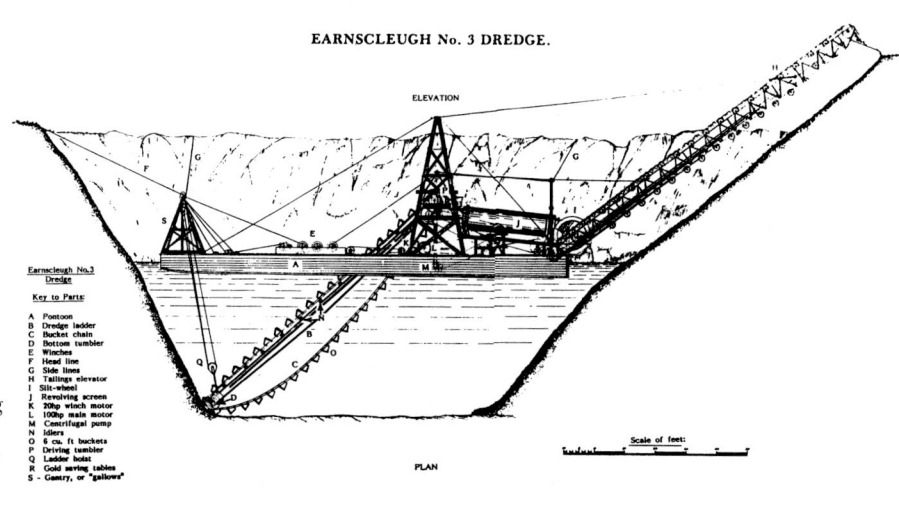

Plan of a typical New Zealand dredge working in its dredge pond at Earnscleugh Flat. *AJHR*, 1901.

be successful, and the operations of the early machines at least appeared to justify close attention to the development of the dredging theory. The answer, of course, was the application of steam power.

The early stream-driven bucket and ladder dredges were not very successful in returning gold until Choie Sew Hoy put a small one on Big Beach on the Lower Shotover River. By July 1889 it was winning "large quantities of gold for its fortunate shareholders",[1] which stimulated a 'gold dredging boom' in Otago.

During the 1890s the "Standard" or "New Zealand dredge" was developed and became internationally renowned. The buckets delivered the spoil into either a sluice box with riffles to trap the gold, or a revolving cylinder with perforations, where the gold-bearing wash fell onto gold saving tables and mats. Initially this screened gravel, or tailings, was simply dumped by a chute off the stern. But this resulted in the riverbed becoming fouled by an overburden of tailings. So a tailings elevator was invented, with a conveyor belt to systematically stack the gravel as far away as possible from the orbit of the dredge.

By 1899 there were 94[1] dredges at work with 37 new ones under construction. Some gold dredging companies did better than others, the two most successful being the "Electric" and "Hartley and Riley [sic] Beach".

The 'electric' dredges that weren't electric!

In 1895 the Electric Gold Dredging Co. was formed with a partnership that included Alexander ("Alec") McGeorge, his two brothers and Charles Coote, a traveller for a product called "Electric Essence". Jocularly, Coote had suggested the name "Electric" for the company and the name stuck. The company's first dredge, Electric No. 1, was constructed off the mouth of the Bannockburn. At first the little dredge didn't do well. Then, as Alec McGeorge's biographer[2] relates, when Alec joined the dredge one of the winchmen pointed out that a horseshoe nailed above the boiler-house door was hanging upside down. "No wonder you have been unlucky", the winchman proclaimed. The goodluck symbol was restored to the correct and efficacious position as accepted by the superstitious. It is possible that by this simple act and no other, that a whole new chapter opened up for the gold dredging industry. More likely it was Alec's special knowledge of the Clutha River and that he shifted the little dredge down to the gold-rich Cornish Point, that it began to do well. In one week of May 1894 the gold wash up was 100 ounces and the next week, 235 ounces.

With these sort of returns the company built a second dredge, *Electric No. 2* and then a third, *Electric No. 3*. The latter was much larger and more powerful than its two predecessors and was constructed at Scotland Point. The launching date, 12 March 1898, just 'happened' to coincide with the visit of Governor-General Lord Ranfurly and his wife to Cromwell and Alec and his brother Joseph ("Joe"), the dredgemaster, managed to persuade the Governor to christen the dredge, *Lady Ranfurly*, after his wife.[2]

> "Alec and his brother drove the Governor and his retinue to the Kawarau Gorge, followed by the great majority of the inhabitants of Cromwell in every conceivable sort of vehicle. On the way to the launching site, Joe McGeorge requested the Governor-General to christen the dredge and this he agreed to do. The traditional bottle of wine was broken over the pontoon by Mrs James McGeorge, the only McGeorge wife present, and Lord Ranfurly formally named the dredge-to-be the *Lady Ranfurly*. The dredge's good future was toasted in the workmen's hut nearby, Joseph McGeorge having wisely made provision accordingly."

Lady Ranfurly dredge (Electric No. 3) working off Scotland Point, Kawarau River, where she made her record returns. *Alexandra Museum*

The New Zealand Dredge 171

Lady Ranfurly's world record return in 1902 of 1,234 ounces of gold in one week. James McGeorge, far left. *Alexandra Museum*

Mounted boiler of the famous *Lady Ranfurly* dredge, Domain Road, Bannockburn.

In this way the prosaically named *Electric No. 3* got the glamorous name-change which suited its charmed future. Auspiciously, within its first four weeks of operations off Scotland Point she netted nearly 800 ounces of gold. Her fortunes continued and in July 1902 she returned 1,234 ounces of gold in one week, a world record at that time. This bettered the previous record of that other highly successful dredge, the *Hartley and Riley* [sic], which, in March 1900 returned 1,187[3] ounces of gold in an equivalent period of one week.

The *Lady Ranfurly* continued on her winning ways, breaking her own record in 1906 with a return of 1,273 ounces of gold in under five days. By 1918, however, she had run out of gold. After lying idle for some time off Scotland Point,[2] her 'birthplace' and the spot where she had made her record returns, she caught on fire and was dragged onto the beach. The remains of her ironworks could be seen there for many years, but these have now been flooded over and silted up.

Hartley and Riley dredge battling its way up the Clutha River at Cromwell, 1899. The dredge made its best returns off Hartley's Beach, below Cromwell. *Alexandra Museum*

New Zealand's first electric dredge, the *Sandhills* dredge, working in the upper Shotover River, 1891. *Alexandra Museum*

Maori Point cutter-suction dredge in 1926. Note tall diving bell on right. *Alexander Turnbull Library*

The boiler from the famous dredge has been mounted on a stand on Domain Road at Bannockburn.

Her rival in success, the *Hartley and Riley*, worked the fabled beach where the original prospectors, Hartley and Reilly (the correct spelling)[4] had taken their 87 pounds of gold, and after whom the dredge had been named, albeit misspelling Reilly's name. Robert Gilkison[3] tells the story of how the dredge had a lean time at first and then she had a lucky accident:

> "For some time she worked down to a hard cement bottom from twenty to forty feet below the water, and earned only small returns. It was owing to a lucky accident that a great discovery was made. One night, at the black hour of twelve, a man came on board to work the 'graveyard shift'. He had been drinking, and not having proper control over himself, began work by letting the ladder go down with a jerk. As luck would have it, the blow given by the ladder broke through the cement, and before long the buckets were bringing up rich gold from underneath. That incident was the beginning of the big returns. The Hartley dredge never got poor returns again until the claim was worked out."

By 1900 New Zealand dredges had won international renown. Engineer William McKinnon from British Columbia was just one of a number of overseas visitors intent on learning what they could of the newborn dredging industry and he wrote:[2]

> "The District of Otago, at the South end of the Middle Island, has become the Mecca to which the engineer in search of information on the subject directs his pilgrimage. The writer lately paid a visit to the town of Alexandra, in Otago, for the purpose of seeing for himself the operation of dredging for gold and studying the conditions, with the view of applying the same means to recovering gold from the rivers and gravel beds of British Columbia. Within a distance of five miles from Alexandra, some twenty dredges are at work on the Clutha River and Manuherikia Creek . . . The industry has now become such a success that the New Zealand appliances are being copied for use in other parts of the world. Dredges are at the present time being built for use in Siberia . . ."

Truly electric dredges

The last significant development in dredging was the use of hydro-electric power to drive the machinery. The first electric dredge was built on the Sandhills claim[4] on the upper Shotover River in 1891. A surprisingly remote area for this first model, but New Zealand's first hydro-electric power station was in the vicinity and the local miners at Bullendale were quick to realise the suitability of electricity to power dredges.

Water was drawn from Stony Creek (a tributary of the Shotover River) and conveyed to a generator house set up beside the river.[4] But large parts of the Sandhills claim had already been worked by other methods and there was not sufficient virgin ground to allow the dredge to work at a profit. Accordingly, in 1899 the Sandhills dredge was dismantled and removed to Millers Flat, near Roxburgh, where a number of dredges worked.

The owners of the Maori Point dredge also drew water from Stony Creek for their power plant at Maori Point. Launched in 1926[4] it was a remarkable cutter-suction dredge and had a diving bell. But the rotating cutter head was unable to cope with the boulders and not surprisingly, the suction intake soon blocked with schist. At its trials a penny was thrown overboard and later recovered from the tables, prompting one visitor to observe that it was "indeed a remarkable machine, it had even changed the date on the penny"! Also the use of the diving bell "did not disclose any coarse gold in the crevices". In spite of reassurances from various 'experts', the dredge proved a failure. Nevertheless, the massive iron superstructure of the Maori Point dredge is one of the most visible remains of a dredge today.[5] Recently, using modern machinery, Maori Point has been reworked with much greater success than its predecessor.

Power plants sprang up whenever needed by a dredge and the original Fraser Dam station[4] was constructed for the *Earnscleugh No. 3* dredge. A paddock dredge designed to work in a pond away from the river, it was the largest dredge to be built at that time (1902). For over twenty years it worked successfully on Earnscleugh Flat, leaving a great mountain of tailings on the flat in the process. In 1926, when it came to the end of its very profitable time on the flat, it was shifted to the Upper Nevis Valley, uplifting its two generators from the Fraser power station and setting them up in the valley.

The huge, but unprofitable, *Molyneux* dredge passing beneath the Bannockburn Bridge. *Courtesy Ron Murray*

Earnscleugh No. 3 dredge, which worked successfully at Earnscleugh Flat for over 20 years. In 1926 it was shifted, with its power plant, to the upper Nevis Valley. *Alexandra Museum*

Molyneux anchored downstream from the remains of the famous *Lady Ranfurly* dredge at Scotland Point. *R. S. M. Sinclair*

Three giants

During the mid-1900s three enormous dredges worked the Clutha River and its tributaries, drawing their electric power from the Roaring Meg and Fraser River stations. The drain on the power for the region was so great that when one of them hit a boulder during the night shift the lights of Queenstown dipped![5]

Built at Clyde in 1936, the *Molyneux* was by far the largest and most powerful dredge to work the river.[6]

It dredged from Clyde to Kawarau Gorge in a remarkably brief period, and at Kawarau Gorge it still [1951] sits, a beautiful machine with nothing to do. It probably established a long distance speed record for dredges over river courses, and its crew certainly performed wonders in getting through the narrow rocky gorges, over river bars and under bridges, but that is little consolation to the shareholders. The astonishing thing about this dredge is not that it failed – for that was a foregone conclusion – but that it got so little gold. While conceding that the boom period dredges made a pretty good job, it is difficult to accept the evidence that they were so thorough that practically nothing remained.

The *Molyneux's* twin, the *Clutha,* which dredged successfully at Earnscleugh Flat from 1940 to 1962. *R. S. M. Sinclair*

The giant *Lowburn* dredge which worked the Clutha River from Cromwell to Lowburn from 1940 to 1952, when it was exported to Malaya to dredge for tin. *Alexander Turnbull Library*

The vast sea of tailings at Earnscleugh Flat. Dredge ponds in foreground.

Having completed her marathon 'speed record' from Clyde to the Kawarau Gorge, the *Molyneux* lay moored for ten years downstream from her famous predecessor, the *Lady Ranfurly*. Then in 1953 she was sold for scrapmetal.

The *Clutha* (1904-62) was a twin to the *Molyneux* and was soon converted to a paddock dredge to work Earnscleugh Flat. Equipped with a tailings elevator it worked there until 1962, adding greatly to the mountain of tailings left by its predecessors, *Earnscleugh No. 2* and *No. 3* and others.

This vast sea of dredged gravel has now been preserved as the Earnscleugh Tailings Reserve. These long gravel ridges increase in height the further you move away from the river and smother a once rich orchard and some earlier sluice tailings. Rusting relics of the dredges will be found amongst the tailings and also dredge ponds where they once worked. Enter the reserve from Marshall Road and climb the track to the top of the tailings to gain an overall view of this vast sea of tailings. Then walk the Otago Regional Council's new riverwalk, which extends from Alexandra to Clyde.

The largest dredge of all and indeed one of the largest built in the world was the huge 3,300 ton Austral-New Zealand Co's dredge, *Lowburn*. Launched in 1940 she worked the Clutha River from Cromwell up to Lowburn. In its first eight years of operations it recovered just under 73,000 ounces of gold. Then, with a fall-off in returns, she was dismantled in 1952 and exported to Malaya to dredge for tin.

So ended the remarkable era of dredging the Clutha River and its tributaries for gold. An era now gone, but the Clutha survives and still flows on down to the sea. Civis of the *Otago Daily Times* puts it neatly in his delightful adaption of Tennyson's *The Brook*.[7]

> Through many a gorge I roar and race
> With many a breaker cutting
> By many a jutting rocky face
> In many an eddy swirling.
>
> Then out I shoot with arrowy sweep
> To fill my bends and reaches,
> To slip through channels smooth and deep,
> And spread along my beaches.
>
> By old-time camps I hurry down,
> By worked-out scarps and ledges;
> Then strike a brand-new dredging town
> And half a hundred dredges.

I chuckle, chuckle, as I flow –
The changeless golden river!
For mining crazes come and go,
But I go on for ever.

I surge about the dredger's keel,
Her straining guys and anchor;
I drive the groaning current-wheel,
I follow up the banker.

I lap the buckets as they lift
To light my golden gravel;
I spread along my bed the drift
Of tailings as I travel.

And still I chuckle as I flow –
Th' exhaustless golden river!
For booms may come and booms may go,
But I go on for ever.

Extract

REFERENCES
1. Hearn, T. J. and Hargreaves, R. P., *the Speculators' Dream*, 1985
2. Sinclair, R. S. M., *Kawarau Gold*, 1962
3. Gilkison, Robert, *Early Days in Central Otago*, 1930
4. Chandler, Peter and Hall, R., *Let There Be Light*, 1986
5. Hamel, Jill, *The Archaeology of Otago*, 2001
6. Parcell, J. C., *Heart of the Desert*, 1951
7. Civis, *The Brook*, Otago version, *Otago Daily Times*, 23/9/1899.

Index

Bold figures indicate illustrations

Advance Peak **104,** 110
Ah Lum, **112,** 113-114
Ah Wak, **113,** 113
Alexandra, **37, 38,** 40, 65
All Nations battery, **109,** 108
Alpine Reef battery, **52, 53,** 52
Andersons battery, **107,** 107, 108
Archibald, T., 9
Arthur, T., **116,** 115
Arthurs Point, 115
Arrow River, 101-112
Arrowtown, **102, 103,** 101, 112-114
Arrowtown's Chinatown, **112-114,** 112-114
Aspinall, J., **117,** 119-120, 129
Aultbea Hotel, 158

Bailey, J., 81
Baileys Hill, **83,** 81
Bald Hill (Fruitlands), **44, 45,** 43-46
Balderson, M., 127
Baldwin, W., 21-22
Bannockburn, **75,** 74-76, 79
Bannockburn sluicings, **75,** 76
Barry, J., 75-76
battery, workings of a, **138,** 137
Beale brothers, 104
Beaumont, **65,** 63, 65
Becks, **62,** 63
Bell-Kilgour mine, **137,** 137
Bendigo, **87,** 86-92
Bennetts, J., **47, 49,** 50
berdan, workings of a **78, 139,** 140
Black Horse brewery, **23,** 24
Blacks (Ophir), **156, 157,** 156-157
Blue Spur, **26, 27,** 18-19, 24-26
Booth, R., 13
Bordeau, J., **128, 129,** 129
Box, S., 86-87
Bracken, 33, 103
Bremner, J., **147-149,** 158, 161
Buchanan, J., 11, 71
Bullen, G., 122, 124
Bullen Hall, **125,** 122-124
Bullendale, **120-125,** 120-125
Burgess R., **33,** 33
Butchers Gully, **42,** 42
Butchers Gully Hotel, **42,** 42

Callery, J., **165,** 165
Callerys' battery, **164,** 165
Campbell brothers, 46
Campbells Creek, **47,** 46-47, 50
Cambrians, **152, 153,** 151-153
Canton battery, **31,** 31

Cape Broom Hotel, **44,** 44
Cardrona, **95-99,** 94-99
Cardrona Hotel, **97, 98,** 97, 99
Cargill, J., 19, 39, 43
Cargill, W., **10,** 9-10
Carrick Range mines, 75-79
Carrick water race, **76,** 77-78
Carricktown, 76-78
Chamonix, 50
Chandler, P., **49,** 49
Charlestown, 117
Chinese Empire Hotel, **28,** 27-28
Choie Sew Hoy, **168,** 169
Choie Sew Hoy's dredge, **169,** 169
Clutha dredge, **175,** 177
Clutha (Molyneux) River, **38, 57, 72,** 9, 168, 177-178
Clyde, **39, 40, 67,** 40, 68
Cobb & Co., **42, 67,** 58-67, 134, 156
Come in Time battery, **91,** 91
Conroys Gully, **41,** 41-43
Cormack, J., 101-102
Cornish, E., 74
Cornish Point, **71, 74,** 70, 74, 170
Consolidated battery, **166,** 167
Cordts, N., 49
Criffel diggings, **100,** 100
Cromwell, **71-73,** 40, 68-73
Cromwell's Chinatown, **71,** 71
Cruickshank, G., 135
Crystal battery, **127,** 126

Dansey Pass, 161
Dansey Pass Hotel, **160, 161,** 161-162
Dart River dredge, **141,** 142
Docherty W., 15, 71
Doctors Point, **53, 54,** 52-54
Don, A., **30, 139, 156,** 48, 156
Donaldsons' battery, **165,** 163-164
Drybread, **149, 150,** 149
Dugan, G., 47
Duncan, M., **117,** 117, 119
Dunstan (Clyde), **39, 40,** 68
Dunstan (Cromwell) Gorge, **38, 39, 68-70,** 35-40, 68-70
Dunstan Mts, **38,** 35
Dunstan Road, **59, 61,** 58-63
Dunstan rush, 34-41
Dwyer, E., 49-51
Dynamo Flat, **124,** 123, 125

Earnscleugh station, 37
Earnscleugh tailings, **177,** 177
Earnscleugh No. 3 dredge, **84, 168, 175,** 84, 174
Ellison, D., **116,** 116-117

Evans, F., 122
Ewing, J., 155

Flynn, J., 120
Fox, W., **102,** 94, 101-103, 111
Foxs (Arrowtown), 95, 101
Fraser, H., **165,** 165
Fraser, W., 37, 68
Fraser River, **52, 53,** 51-53
Fruitlands (Bald Hill), **44, 45,** 43-46

Gabriels Gully, **18, 20, 21, 24-25,** 16-26, 63
Galloway, **60,** 60
Galvin, P., **99,** 99
Garibaldi, **158,** 158
Garvie, A., 11, 71
Garvey, **162,** 162-163
Garrett, W., 88, 91
Gay Tan, **164,** 163
Gee's Flat, 137, 139
George, E., **160,** 161-162
German Hill, **157, 158,** 157-158
Gilkison, R., 134, 173
Gillies, J., 17, 19, 21
Glenore, **11,** 11
Golden Point, **164, 165,** 163-166
Golden Progress mine, **160,** 159-160
Goodger, G., **88,** 88-91
Goodger, M., 89
Goodger Flat, 13, 15
Gordon, H. A., 119, 123
Gordon Creek monument, **51,** 51
Griffiths, G., 149
Grogan, M., 94

Haeroa, H., 116-117
Halfway House, **69,** 68
Hamel, J., 166
Hamilton, A., 149, 151
Hamilton, J., 147
Hamiltons, **148,** 147-148
Hardy, J., 17-19
Harris, J. H., 144, 149
Hartley, H., 34-37, 40, 173
Hartleys Beach, **35, 36,** 37, 40
Hartley and Riley dredge, **35, 172,** 171, 173
Hassing, G., **94,** 15, 68, 71-72, 86-87, 95-97
Hebden, B., 88, 91
Hector, J., 94, 103
Hogburn (see Naseby)
Hogburn Gully, **145, 146,** 144-147
Holloway, 100
Horseshoe Bend, **55,** 55-56
Homeward bound battery, **109,** 108, 109

Hyde, **149,** 148, 149

Invincible battery, **139-141,** 139-141

Jenkins, W., **106,** 107
Johnston, S., 120
Joss House, **27, 28,** 27-28

Kawarau dam, **136,** 134-137
Kawarau Gorge Mining Centre, **138, 139,** 137-139
Kawarau River, **135, 136, 138,** 134-138
Keddell, J., 40-41, 60
Kelly, T., **33,** 33
Kemp, J., **44,** 43, 44
Kildare Hill, **156,** 155
Knobby Range Road, **64,** 65
Kwong Wye Kee, **32,** 31
Kyeburn diggings, **160, 161,** 161-163

Lady Ranfurly dredge, **170, 171, 175,** 170-171
La Franchi, A., 97
La Franchi's dredge, **96,** 97
Lawrence, **20, 28, 29,** 26-29
Lawrence's Chinatown, **27, 28,** 26-29
Lees Stream Hotel, **58,** 58
Leviathan battery, **127,** 126
Levy, P., **33,** 33, 158
Ligar, C., 10, 17
Lindis Hotel, **14,** 15
Lindis Pass, **12,** 12
Lindis rush, 12-15
Loch Linnhe station, **82,** 81
Logan, T., 87-89
Logan's (Cromwell) reef, **90,** 88
Logantown, **88,** 89, 91
Lonely graves, **56,** 56
Low, T., 101
Lowborn dredge, **176,** 177
Lye Bow, **43,** 43
Lysaght, P., **38,** 39

McArthur, V., 125, 130
McCraw, J., 41, 42 50
McDougall, R., **96,** 97, 100
McGeorge brothers, **171,** 170
McGregor, J., **101,** 101
McLean, G., 81-83
McLean, I., 81
McLean, J., 13
McNeur, G., **32, 110**
Macnicol, A., **127,** 120, 126
McPhee's Hotel, 59
Macraes, **163, 164,** 163-164
MacTavish, L., **156,** 157
Mace brothers, 103-105
Macetown, **104-107,** 103-107, 111-112
Manuherikia River, **37, 38, 57,** 11, 35
Maori Point, **116, 173,** 116-117, 174
Maori Point dredge, **173,** 174
Matakanui (see Tinkers)
Matilda battery, **90,** 89-92
Menzies, D., **76,** 76
Mitchell, A., **45,** 44-46
Mitchell, J., **46, 47,** 44-46
Mitchells cottage, **46, 47,** 45-46
Moa Creek, **143, 144,** 143-144
Moa Creek Hotel, **60,** 60
Moa Creek, **132, 133,** 131-132
Moke Creek dredge, **132,** 132
Molyneux dredge, **174, 175,** 175-177
Money, C., 21
Moonlight Creek, 131
Moonlight, G., **132,** 131
Mt Aurum, **127,** 119-120
Mt Burster (Buster), 147-148
Mt Morgan Sluicing Co., 151

Mt Pisa, **99,** 100
Munro, G., **17,** 17
Munros Gully, 17
Murray, R., 79, 81, 87, 136, 174
Mutton Town, 68

Nairn, C., **10,** 9
Nairn, F., **38,** 39
Naseby, **145-147,** 144-147
Needham, J., **107,** 107
Nenthorn, **166, 167,** 166-167
Nevis Crossing, 80
Nevis Crossing Hotel, **79,** 80
Nevis, 79-84
Nevis Hotel, **81,** 80
Ng, J., **144,** 26, 29, 143
Ngapara No. 2 dredge, **84**
Nokomai, **85,** 84
Nugget battery, **126,** 126

Oasis Hotel, **59,** 59
Oceana Gold, **165,** 166
Olsen, A., 120
Ophir, **156, 157,** 156-157
OPQ battery, **29,** 30, 109
Otago Hotel, **119,** 119-120, 130
Otuherua, **160,** 159-160
Oxenbridge brothers, 133
Oxenbridge Tunnel, **133,** 133

Parcell, J. C., 92
Parker brothers, **144,** 144
Patearoa (Sowburn), **148,** 148
Paterson, J., **97,** 97
Pengelly's Hotel, **89,** 89, 92
Petchey, P., 111, 124
Peters, E., **11, 16,** 11
Phoenix battery, **120, 121,** 122-124
Phoenix Hotel, **120, 125,** 125
Pigroot, **62,** 60-63
Pigroot Hotel, **62,** 63
Pinchers Bluff, **129,** 130
Pipeclay Terraces, **75,** 75
Pitt, W., **48,** 48
Potter, J. L., **48,** 46, 48
Potters No. 1, **80,** 46, 80
Potters No. 2, **47,** 46, 48
Premier battery, **110,** 107, 110
Prince, W., 123
Pyke, V., **34,** 9-10, 34, 88

Quartz Reef Point, **93,** 92
Quartzville, 76
Queenstown, **140,** 115, 134
Queenstown Bay, **115,** 115

Rakiraki, **9,** 9
Read, G., **17,** 17-22
Ree, A., **49,** 49
Rees, W. G., 101, 115-116
Reilly, C. 34-37, 173
Rich Burn reefs, **107,** 107-110
Richardson, J., 18
Rigney, W., **56,** 56
Ritchie, N., 70-71, 113
Roaring Meg, **95,** 95, 99
Robinson, H., 50
Robertson, P., 19
Rocky Point Hotel, **86,** 86
Romans, M., 113
Roxburgh, **66, 67,** 65
Sam Chew Lain, **28, 29** 28-29
Sandhills dredge, **172,** 174
Scoles, W., **110,** 111
Scotland Point, **137, 170, 175,** 137, 171
Seffers, J., 132
Sefferstown, **132,** 132
Serpentine, **159,** 156-159

Serpentine battery, **159,** 159
Serpentine church, **159,** 158
Sew Hoy, D., **144,** 143
Shotover House, 116
Shotover River, 116
Sinclair, R., 168
Skippers, **117-120,** 117-120
Skippers bridge, **118, 128, 130,** 128, 130
Skippers cemetery, **120,** 120
Skippers Point (Skippers), **117-120,** 119-120
Skippers Road, **128-131,** 128-131
Skippers Sluicing Co., **118,** 119
Smith, T., 106
Smith's bakery, **106,** 106
Solway battery, 89
Southberg battery, 122, 125
Sowburn (Patearoa), **148,** 148
Stanleys Hotel, **163,** 163
St Bathans, **153-156,** 152-156
St Bathans Lake, **155,** 155-156
Stebbing, H., **37,** 37
Stewart, J., **76,** 76
Stewart, J. 51, 51
Stewart Town, **76,** 76
Styx, **59, 60,** 60
Sunrise mine, 110
Swan brewery, **70,** 70
Symes, R., 45

Teviot, **66,** 54-55, 65
Teviot station, **64,** 63
Tewa, J., 101
The Junction (see Cromwell), 71
Thomson, J., 16
Thomson, J. T., **12,** 11-12, 19, 21, 35, 57-58, 73, 95, 100, 128
Thompson, W., **91,** 91
Tinkers (Matakanui), **149-151,** 149-151
Tipperary battery, **108,** 107, 108
Trollope, A., 67
Tunnel claim, **47,** 46-47
Twelve Apostles, **104,** 105-106

United Goldfields battery, **109,** 108

Victory battery, **30,** 30
Vogel, J., 134-135

Waipori, **32,** 31-32
Waipori River, **32,** 31-32
Waitahuna, **22,** 22
Wakefield, **86,** 86-87
Weatherston, B., 23
Weatherston brothers, 22-23
Weatherstons, **22, 23,** 22-24
Welcome Home Hotel, **131,** 131
Welshtown, **89,** 89, 91
White, J., **45,** 44
White Horse Hotel, **62,** 63
Williamson, J., **85,** 84
Wilson, 100
Wood, J., 59, 149
Woodhouse, J., **54,** 54

Young, A., **54,** 54
Young Australian mine, **77, 78,** 78

Text: 10/10.5 New Baskerville
Paper: 128gsm gloss art
Book jacket: 128gsm gloss art
Book design: Ellen van Empel
Bound by S. I .McHarg Bookbinders, Christchurch, NZ
Printed by Craig Printing Company Limited, Invercargill, NZ